Poetry:
Tools & Techniques

*A Practical Guide to Writing
Engaging Poetry*

John C. Goodman

Gneiss Press

Published by Gneiss Press, BC, Canada
www.gneisspress.com

Library and Archives Canada Cataloguing in Publication

Goodman, John C. (John Charles), 1951-
    Poetry : tools and techniques : a practical guide to writing
engaging poetry / John C. Goodman.

Issued also in electronic formats.
ISBN 978-0-9869657-2-2

    1. Poetry--Authorship. I. Title.

PN1059.A9G66 2011   808.1   C2011-907156-8

DEDICATION

This book is for everyone who believes that poetry isn't confined to the critically accepted works on library shelves, but is a vital experience, a living movement, a heartbeat, a dance, a rock concert.

CONTENTS

Poetry:
Tools & Techniques
A Practical Guide to Writing
Engaging Poetry

1

Introduction

In spite of the industrial sounding title, *Poetry Tools & Techniques*, writing poetry is not a mechanical process, it is a creative process, but there are structural elements to writing that every poet needs to know. As editor of a poetry magazine I receive numerous submissions from beginning poets. It seems that many new writers aren't really sure what they are doing. They write what they feel, imitating the style of other poets without really understanding the background and mechanics of the techniques they are using.

I felt the need for a little handbook on the basics of writing poetry, an introduction to the nitty-gritty mechanisms of language, the actual techniques and devices that go into making a poem, right down to the nuts and bolts structural parts of language – the conjunctions, prepositions, articles, etc. – and how they affect poetic language. It's a short book because I wanted to give a brief overview and not get bogged down in too much detail – the topic of metaphor alone could take up an entire volume. The book, therefore, is more of a starting point for writers to find their own directions than a definitive textbook on how to write in the proper and approved manner. Each poet really needs to read critically and figure things out for him or herself. Learning the techniques and devices illustrated in this book will help in the critical analysis of the work of other poets and contribute to the overall understanding of poetry.

In this book we will investigate the structure of language and how it conveys meaning – and from that learn how to create and use a poetic, a philosophy of language, to shape and inform our writing. We will explore the limits of language and discover how to make language speak beyond itself – to make language say what it was not designed to say, to express the inexpressible.

There will be writers who vehemently disagree with some of the approaches taken in this book – and that's a good thing. We don't want to be clones following the same rules and regulations, churning out the same type of turgid verse. Poetry isn't what anyone tells you it "should" be; poetry is what you, as a writer, make it.

There are many styles of poetry, from formal to experimental, but an understanding of the basic techniques is essential for any style – even if it means that you reject the traditional devices entirely and try for something new. The examples in this book are mainly free verse, but the same fundamental principles apply to formal and experimental poetry. This is not a book of writing exercises, but a book of ways to help you improve your craft.

Most of the example quotes are drawn from works that can be readily found in any standard anthology of English poetry or online and so are easily available and accessible to anyone who wants to follow up with further reading.

– John C. Goodman

ditch, (www.ditchpoetry.com)

2

Poetic Language

This is a book about the mechanics of poetry in which we will be considering the nuts and bolts elements that go into making a poem and how to combine them into workable verse. Poetry is first and foremost about language, for language is the medium of poetry – in the same way that paint is the medium of visual art. If a poem is written in original and engaging language it can be about practically anything and be in any form and still be successful poetry. Our most compelling poetry fuses the language, the form and the content together, just like ingredients are blended together in a recipe to allow the different flavours to enhance each other and make for a delicious overall taste; or the way the parts of a machine are assembled together to make an elegant and workable mechanism. Attaining this synchronicity of elements is what we will be working towards.

Language is the medium of poetry and mastering language is the task of the poet. You wouldn't expect a musician to get up on stage who hadn't learned to play an instrument; you wouldn't expect to see paintings hung in a gallery by an artist who had not learned how to mix and apply the paint. In the same way, don't expect to see poetry published by a writer who has not taken the time to master the medium of poetry: language. It may seem that we are constantly practising with language since we use it in conversation every day, but conversational language is very different from poetic language. Developing a poetic language requires study, practice and skill.

3

The Limits of Language

Language has limits and poets are continually encountering the stormy edges of communication. For an example of the limits of language, suppose you met someone suffering from protanopia, red colour-blindness, and wanted to describe to them the colour red. How would you do it? Usually when we describe something we resort to comparisons: red as a rose, fire engine red, blood red, etc., but these would be meaningless to someone who does not know what red is in the first place. The fact is that it is impossible to convey the concept of 'red.'

You may attempt to give an impression by relating it to things the other person already knows, such as saying that red is a hot colour or an angry colour or like some of Stravinsky's music, but that still doesn't express the essence of red, the quality of redness, what a red object looks like. Red in and of itself can only be experienced, it cannot be described by language. The same is true of any colour, sound, taste, smell or touch sensation. The point is that all our basic perceptual experience, our fundamental apprehension of reality, is beyond the scope of language. How then do we communicate?

Most of our ability to communicate depends on a shared reality – we can only talk about things of which the other person has some experience. We can extend the range of our communication through extrapolation and exaggeration as in phrases such as, "sweeter than a nightingale's song in spring" – you may never have heard a nightingale sing in spring, but you get the idea that it is something pretty sweet, sweeter than anything in your own experience, and so you are led to imagine something outside the limits of what you know.

Now, a nightingale's song in spring is something real that you could possibly hear if you were in the right place at the right time and so it is still an element of our common world. But there are some things personal and private to ourselves that no one else can ever experience. Our own inner feelings of joy, sorrow, delight and pain are unique to each of us and cannot be directly felt by anyone else.

Expressing our emotions is difficult because our language isn't designed to deal with anything that isn't solid. Our language is structured to talk about things in the external world, about objects. Consider how we deal with nothing. Nothing is, by definition, not a thing, it is no-thing, yet we talk about nothing as if it were something. Suppose someone said to you, "I had nothing for breakfast," and someone else said, "I had porridge for breakfast." There is a great deal of difference between nothing and porridge, but our language treats them exactly the same, the sentence structure, "I had ____ for breakfast," is the same whether you have something or nothing. In language, nothing is treated as if it were something.

The only way our language allows us to talk about non-things is to treat them like physical objects, yet a vast part of our experience of the world doesn't exist objectively. Emotions, colours, sounds, tastes, sensations, absences, qualities, attributes, space, time, music, feelings, all have to be treated like objects. So how do we talk about a thing that is not a thing? How do we communicate our emotions? Can we write unobjectively? How do we objectify a feeling? How do we make the language say something it was not designed to say?

Again, we most often resort to comparisons. Ornery as a mule, angry as a bag of snakes, miserable as a dog with no bone, are common ways of expressing personal attributes. But besides references to the outside world, we can evoke a shared inner reality as well. We can assume that almost everyone has experienced some degree of happiness or hurt or loneliness or fulfilment or disappointment as these are all part of the human condition. Such feelings can be expressed through images or word pictures that convey an impression of the writer's inner experience.

How to communicate the ephemeral is one of the difficulties of language that writers have struggled with since the earliest English poetry. In the Old English poem *A Woman's Lament*, we find,

> Alone I sing of my journey into sadness,
> A song that is mine alone..."

A journey, which is a physical movement from one place to another, is used to describe a non-physical, emotional investigation into feelings of sorrow and loneliness. The description of what isn't in terms of what is, of making the language speak beyond itself, is one of the basic challenges of the English language. The approaches writers have taken to solve this, and other problems of language, have determined what we call poetry.

The whole purpose of this book is to explore the limits of language and to find ways around those limits; to find ways of expressing the inexpressible.

4

Working with a Poetic

Poems don't just happen, they are made. All the significant poetry in the history of English literature was written to a poetic. A poetic is the set of guidelines or parameters or restraints or constraints that direct the writer's intention. The poetic determines the placement on the page of every word, every line break, every punctuation mark, every space. Serious poets don't simply write what they feel, they work with a poetic, they write what they feel with intention.

A poetic is a series of ideas about how language can be utilized in a unique way to convey the poet's unique point of view. It is a philosophy about how to communicate through language. A poetic doesn't have to be an iron-clad, strictly defined set of rules, it can be as amorphous, diffuse and fuzzy around the edges as you want, but the writer's poetic is what gives direction and continuity to the work. It's the map that allows you to follow the paths of your creativity; it's the toolbox of techniques and devices that will help you express your distinctive voice.

If you read the history of English poetry from Chaucer to our present day writers, you will see that many different approaches to the art and craft of poetry have been explored. There are endless ways in which the elements of poetry can be combined and language can be manipulated. Poets have written formal verse, free verse, open form, Surrealist poetry, Romantic poetry, urban poetry, lyric poetry, political critiques, love poetry, social commentary and much, much more. With all these styles, types, forms and varieties of content available, how do we choose what is the best way to write? For an answer to that question, we turn to our poetic.

5

Adventures in Language:
Syntax, Words and Meaning

We can find an example of a poetic in action in this little poem:

On the Riprap at Six Mile Beach

The vision of smiles in the holiday throng;
Ripples on a still deep pond.

The poet could have written,

The holidaymakers' smiles shimmer
Like ripples on a still deep pond.

but he deliberately left out the word 'like' that would normally link the two images together. He did this in order to create a specific effect. 'Like' is a prepositional conjunction, or connecting word. Language without conjunctions is called disjunctive. Here we can discern part of the writer's poetic: omitting the connecting words, or conjunctions, to make the language disjunctive. The effect of this disjunctive language is to leave the discovery of the connection between the images in the poem to the mind of the reader. Instead of the poet *telling* us that the smiles are like ripples, he simply presents the two incongruent pictures side by side and lets us make the association for ourselves. The disjunctive juxtaposition of clauses is a technique called parataxis.

In this writer's poetic, disjunctive language is important. So are images. Notice that there isn't any narrative in the poem; it doesn't start out, "I was at Six Mile Beach the other day when I observed..." – all the poet does is present the images. So another part of the poetic is to write in a non-narrative style. The poem is also objective, about things in the world around us, rather than subjective, about the narrator himself.

We could then say that this writer's poetic is to write in a disjunctive, non-narrative, objective style centered on images. In order to grasp the poetic we didn't look at just what was there, but what was not there – we noted the absence of conjunctions and narrative. In a poetic, the negative spaces, the missing elements, are just as important as the positive aspects. The negative spaces form the background for the presentation of the devices used; they make the visible elements stand out.

What we have seen here is how ideas about how to write a poem have shaped the final product. The poet didn't write the piece and then realize, "I've just written a non-narrative, disjunctive, objective poem." The idea of writing this style of poetry was in his head before he ever set pen to paper. The writer started with a poetic that shaped his unique way of using language.

[*Further Reading:* for an example of non-narrative, disjunctive, objective poetry, look up *In a Station of the Metro* by Ezra Pound in which he associates the people in a subway station with the blossoms of a flowering tree – without using the conjunction 'like.']

One potential problem with our sample poem is the word 'riprap' in the title. Riprap is the loose stone used to make breakwaters in harbours, but it is not a common term and anyone who is unfamiliar with the meaning could be confused by the word and lose the flow of the line. There is certainly a place for obscure words in poetry, but you have to decide when and where it is best to use them to greatest effect. In this example, if the poet wanted the piece to be more accessible to the reader, he might consider revising the title to *On the Breakwater at Six Mile Beach*.

Uniqueness is an important part of poetry. Imitative, derivative and unoriginal are terms you never want applied to your writing. To be influenced by another writer is different from imitating. Imitative or derivative writing results from an attempt to copy someone else's style or voice. To be influenced by is to build on what has gone before, to take another writer's innovations and use them as the basis for further innovations of your own. Ezra Pound, one of the originators of a style of poetry called Imagism, didn't just sit down one day and say, "I think I'll make up a new way of writing poetry." The development of the Imagist poetic came from a long process of experimentation and the study of other writers.

On the Riprap at Six Mile Beach and Ezra Pound's *In a Station of the Metro* play with the structure of language by omitting the conjunctions. But the structure of language, or syntax, can be just as powerful as the words in conveying meaning. Look at this example from Lewis Carroll's *Jabberwocky*:

'Twas brillig and the slithy toves
Did gyre and gimble in the wabe

Here the words are all made up, but we can still form an impression of what is going on: we know that there are things called toves, which can be described as slithy, and that they can gyre and gimble. Even though the words are nonsense, there are enough of the structural parts of language in the poem to make the sentence appear meaningful. When we are writing poetry, we are not just dealing with words, we are involved with the very structure of language and how it conveys meaning. This is the essence of a poetic.

6

What You Say
and How You Say It

We saw how the poetic behind *On the Riprap at Six Mile Beach* could be expressed as disjunctive, objective, non-narrative and image based – and all this was deduced from a poem of two lines and a title. This gives us an important lesson: when people read your work, they aren't reading just what you say, but how you say it. They are looking at your command of language, your facility with poetic devices, your craft, your originality, your poetic.

A poetic written out might look something like this:

"In my writing I try to evoke the feeling of sensitive emotions assaulted by a hostile reality. I accomplish this by relying on emotionally charged images augmented by striking modifiers and unusual comparisons. I write free verse, mostly in short lines close to the left margin, but sometimes break out into open forms to express the yearning for freedom. I take my inspiration from nature and natural patterns using melodic language that captures the flow of time and the seasons."

Or like this:

"The stress is not on the verse, but on the line. Lines are written in the breath rhythm, the line ending at the natural breath pause, often ending with prepositions. Conjunctions are included only when necessary. Similes are never used, only juxtaposed metaphor. All punctuation is omitted; the pace of the reading is determined by the positioning of lines on the page in an open form. My writing is non-linear and completely objective, never in the first person."

Or this:

"I compress everything into forceful personal narratives drawn from events in my life, writing in abrupt lines that always end in power words. The reader must be engaged in dramatic situations and captured by strong, direct language that shakes the mind out of its complacency and reveals the truth behind the mirage of existence. I rarely use adjectives or adverbs, allowing the nouns and verbs to speak for themselves."

As you can see, each of these three writers has a different vision of language and how it communicates – and so each will write very different poetry. Each writer has made choices on how to use language and these choices will determine how the final poem reads on the page. They also have different approaches to the subject matter of poetry.

A lot of choices about language, as in life, are not made consciously. You probably have a favourite colour – and it isn't something you chose consciously, it is a natural inclination. In the same way, different people will be drawn towards different styles of poetry, some more conventional, some more unconventional. Some people are entranced by disjunctive language, others are repelled by it. So devising a poetic is really feeling your way through language and the different elements that go into evolving a poetic. However, while our subconscious tendencies and innate leanings may steer us in the right direction, there are still a number of conscious choices to be made in the harsh light of day. Unless you know what those choices are you won't be able to make informed decisions about them.

A poetic isn't something that can be reduced to a bulleted checklist as it involves your whole being and your attitudes toward life. It is about finding a language that effectively represents those attitudes. It's a process, an organic growth, an unfolding that flowers into words. In the following pages we will delve into the tools and techniques that go into creating a poetic, beginning with Revising and Polishing. It may seem an unusual choice to start with how to revise a written poem rather than how to write a new poem, but it is important to see how the poetic can be applied to the work as a whole and how a philosophy of language can shape a poem.

7

Revising and Polishing

The creative rush that comes with writing poetry is addictive. The feeling of creation can be so intensely ecstatic that it is easy to understand why the ancient Greeks thought inspiration was a visitation from the gods. The uplifting wave of creativity may initially make you feel as if you have written something amazing – and it probably is amazing within the context of your muse, but how wonderful is it in the cold hard world? Our dazzling creations often need reworking. This is where your craft, your command of language and technique, your poetic, comes into play.

First drafts are often filled with poor wording and clumsy constructions, but poems can be improved with carefully considered revisions. One thing to keep in mind when making revisions is the effect a change in one place can have on the rest of the verse. A poem is a whole, a self-contained unit, which usually requires some internal consistency.

Imagine a first draft like this:

An inconstant wind whisks
across the dawn sky.
My love went away
without a word.
I watch the seagulls circle
over fragile cliffs.

Here we have someone pining over a lost love in a lonely setting. Can we intensify the feeling? There are a number of sentiments being expressed here. We have a feeling of betrayal suggested by 'inconstant.' We have the feeling of loss and the disappointment that the lover left 'without a word.' We have the emotional damage suggested by 'fragile' and the loneliness of someone watching gulls circling cliffs at dawn. Which of these sentiments is most important? What do we want to focus on?

Suppose we approach the poem by revising it to follow up on the silence suggested by the line "without a word." In the poem as it stands, there is a sense change from the auditory, "without a word," to the visual of "I watch." It is possible to keep everything within the realm of hearing:

An inconstant wind whispers
through the dawn.
Without a word
my love went away.
A lone gull laments
over barren cliffs.

This is looking at the poem in a whole new way. We now have a poem based on sounds; the whisking wind now whispers, the circling gull now laments. By concentrating on the sounds, we have accentuated the feeling of loss caused by, not just the lover leaving, but leaving without a word. Notice that the auditory clues – whispers, word, laments – are distributed through the poem on alternate lines instead of being all grouped together. This spreads the hearing sense over the whole poem and contributes to the flow.

As this poem emphasises sounds, we need to pay attention to the sound of the language. It is the resonances of the language that tie the lines together. There are repeated 'w' sounds in the first four lines: **w**ind, **w**hispers, da**w**n, **w**ithout, **w**ord, **w**ent, a**w**ay. The last two lines don't have 'w' sounds, but they are linked to the lines above

17

with the 'a' sounds of an, inconstant, dawn, away, laments and barren. The final lines share the 'l' sounds of love, lone, gull, laments, cliffs. Every line has an 'o' sound near the beginning: inconstant, through, without, love, lone, over.

You can see what we have done here. We started off with a concept of language, which is that the intent of a poem can be expressed, not just through the meaning of the words, but through the sounds of the words. This sonic approach to language is one of the defining elements of the poetic. We then applied this poetic to our draft by adding auditory words, like 'whispers,' and building sets of words with related sounds and tones to augment the effect of the auditory words, such as the alliterative sequence 'lone gull laments.' Notice how the poem has only a few hard consonants, concentrating on soft vowel sounds to accentuate the tenderness of the feelings. We didn't change the setting or the imagery, we still have the dawn, the gulls and the cliffs, but we have a much more unified poem centered around sounds and a much more plaintive expression of loss reflected in language oriented to sounds.

But there was one important earlier step: we reread the draft and decided on the core meaning of the poem, in this case, 'leaving without a word.' In first drafts, the meaning is sometimes muddy because the notion or inspiration of the poem isn't fully formed when we sit down to write. A poem doesn't have to be perfect right out of the box. Revising gives us the chance to bring out the core meaning and make it shine.

If we wanted to take this poem a step further, we could concentrate on the absence of sound caused by the lover leaving without a word:

Without a word
my love went away.
No wind whispers
through the dawn.
No gulls lament
over echoless cliffs.

Is this better or worse? Have we now over-revised and ruined the piece? Sometimes knowing when to stop is important. Often, revising and polishing a poem is much harder work than the initial writing. Every poem can be revised in a number of ways; there is no right or wrong, it is what works best for each particular piece – and what works best depends on your poetic, on the vision of language you bring to your work.

When we revise a poem, we have to view it from a different perspective. When we are involved in writing a poem, we may be deeply inside the emotions, but when we revise it, we have to step outside it and see it as a piece of work that can be changed and reshaped until the language of the poem most nearly reflects the core emotion or inspiration or theme. This is often very difficult to do, especially if you are writing about something that stirs intense emotion, such as love or death. Many writers find it helpful to put their first drafts away for a while and revise them later when the feelings are not so raw.

It is in the revision process that our poetic comes into prominence as the poetic guides how we say what we want to say. What we are doing when we revise and polish a poem is bringing the language in line with our poetic, with our concept of how language best expresses what we wish to communicate.

8

Unnecessary Words and
Finding the Right Verbs

Tightening up the language by erasing unnecessary words is an important part of improving any poem. The occurrence of superfluous words is so common in our everyday language that there is even a name for it: pleonasm. Sometimes the first draft of a poem will contain extra words that are common parts of speech, but are really unnecessary for conveying the meaning. For example, the lines,

> Gulls fly over the harbour.
> I can hear them crying out inside of me.

can be tightened up and made much more direct by removing the 'can' and the 'of':

> I hear them crying out inside me

It takes careful reading and reflection to decide which words are necessary. The phrase "crying out inside me" warrants some consideration. You may think that the "out inside" construction contains a nice contrast of opposites, forming a touching point for the writer's inner and outer worlds. On the other hand, it may sound clumsy and overwritten and would be better presented as "I hear them crying inside me," or "I hear their cries inside me," or, "Their cries quiver within me," or even simplified to, "I hear them crying." Each line holds many possibilities.

[*Further Reading:* Mary Oliver deals with the problem of internal sensing in her poem *At Blackwater Pond* in which the narrator listens to bone-deep whispers.]

Suppose our first draft reads,

The seagulls fly up in the sky,
crying out over the harbour.

On a second reading we can see that 'up in the sky' is redundant and can be eliminated – if the gulls are flying, where else would they be but in the sky? There is no need to lumber your readers with superfluous information they already know.

But that leaves us with "The seagulls fly..." 'Fly' is rather a dull verb, surely we can find something more evocative than that: climb, rise, ascend, circle, soar, wheel, sweep, arc, dance, glide, wing, flap, dither, to list just a few of the more obvious alternatives. We want a verb that matches the emotion we are attempting to convey. 'Ascend,' 'soar,' 'dance' may have associations that are too uplifting if we are trying to write a sad poem. Perhaps 'sweep' would be best due to its rhyming association with 'weep.'

Grey gulls, their cries sharp against
the wind, sweep across the harbour.

There are lots of verbs to choose from and finding the right verbs goes a long way to ensuring the success of the poem. Spending time on the verbs is one of the most important elements of writing poetry.

Verbs are time machines, they locate events in time. Events can be shifted in time by changing the verb tense: the gulls flew, gulls fly, gulls will fly. Suppose our first draft reads:

An inconstant wind whisks
across the dawn sky.
My love went away
without a word.
I watched the gulls circle
over fragile cliffs.

we can immediately see an entanglement: change of tense. The poem starts in the present tense with "wind whisks", then ends in the past tense with "I watched". The past tense, "I watched," may be intended to add a sense of nostalgia, to harken back to the moment the lover left, but unless you have a definite reason for mixing up time and viewing past, present and future as co-existent, it is best to keep each poem within its own time frame and be consistent with verb tenses.

An inconstant wind whisks
across the dawn sky.
My love went away
without a word.
I watch the gulls circle
over sombre cliffs.

We can even omit the 'I watch' to let the image bear the weight of the emotion:

My love went away
without a word.
Weary gulls whirl
over sullen cliffs.

9

Too Much Information

First drafts often contain other clutter that can be excised. Sometimes unnecessary background information and explanation can cloud the purpose of the poem and drain the energy from the core feeling.

> My friend sent me an email that said,
> "I love you when your hair's on fire."

Does the reader really need to know that the message came in an email? While it may be factual that an email was received, are the facts important to the poem? The message can be made more dynamic by cutting out the background story,

> He said, "I love you
> when your hair's on fire."

Anything the reader doesn't really need to know can be cut. In most cases, this strengthens the poem; however it may be your intention to convey a chatty, informal, conversational, immediate style. In other words, in your poetic, the fact that the message was delivered in an email may be important – it makes the poem conversational, as if you were telling something to a friend; it brings the reader into your world, because it immediately informs the reader that you receive emotional messages by email. The 'email' changes the emotional balance of the poem because for someone to say "I love you" electronically is different from saying it in person.

These two presentations show how important it is to work to a poetic. Your poetic directs and informs the words on the page. If your intent is to write chatty, spontaneous poetry, you will write, "My friend sent me an email that said, / 'I love you when your hair's on fire.'"

If you want to write more emotionally intense poetry, you will write, "He said, 'I love you / when your hair is on fire.' " The poetic provides the design concept of your writing as well as being the set of tools and techniques that help you build a poem.

10

Rhythm and Flow

Even conversational, immediate style poetry requires work to make the poem effective. Beat poet Allen Ginsberg, for example, wrote very spontaneous, improvisational poetry, but that spontaneous effect came only after much hard work. Ginsberg rewrote and revised his poems over and over again to improve the flow and rhythm in order to make them sound spontaneous.

Flow and rhythm are important since they are what carry the reader through the poem. How the flow and rhythm are regulated within the poem reveal the poet's skill in controlling the medium. The rhythms of some poems are long and flowing, some are short and choppy – and some poems contain both, depending on the effect the poet is trying to achieve.

Writing formal verse in meter sometimes requires twisting and contorting the language to fit the stresses of the metrical feet. In Romantic poetry, you will often find elisions such as o'er and ne'er in which words are shortened from two syllables to one in order to fit the meter. William Wordsworth made an attempt to write flowing metrical verse that more closely followed the forms of common speech; this led Lord Byron to criticize Wordsworth as "writing poetry as if it were prose." Byron, who wrote convoluted lines such as,

> The sword, the banner, and the field,
> Glory and Greece around us see!

had a very different idea of what the language of poetry should be than Wordsworth who, although he wrote in meter, was not above altering the meter to fit the language, resulting in more natural syntax and rhythms,

> Five years have passed; five summers, with the length
> Of five long winters! and again I hear
> These waters, rolling from their mountain springs

In the mid-nineteenth century, Walt Whitman wrote unmetrical lines that were still very rhythmical, basing his rhythms on the high language of the Bible. With the coming of the 20th century and the gradual acceptance of free verse as a legitimate form, traditional metrical forms were mostly abandoned, although poets continued to write in language that was more rhythmical than ordinary prose. Some poets, such as Marianne Moore, wrote in a consciously unrhythmical style to make the language more conversational and sound truer to common speech. Rather than traditional metrical feet, she based her lines on the number of syllables. The result was poetry that, except for the fact that it is broken into lines, sounds prosaic.

[*Further Reading:* Marianne Moore's poem *Poetry* is an example of syllabic verse that reads rather like normal prose in an attempt to avoid the affectations of formal verse.]

Rhythm can be used to heighten emotional effect. Consider this example,

> To-morrow, and to-morrow, and to-morrow,
> Creeps in this petty pace from day to day,
> And all our yesterdays have lighted fools
> The way to dusty death. Out, out, brief candle!

In this speech from *Macbeth* by William Shakespeare, you can feel the tension caused by the change of rhythm from the flowing opening lines to the staccato, "Out, out, brief candle!" – like a cry in the wilderness. This is how poetry speaks to us beyond words. The meaning of the verse is not just in the words, but is conveyed by the very rhythm of the language. The rhythm change wasn't accidental or because the writer felt like it, rather it was the intentional application of a poetic technique in order to increase the emotional impact of the passage. In other words, using rhythm changes to communicate emotional information is a part of the writer's poetic.

11

Assonance and Alliteration

Notice also how the rhythm of Macbeth's speech is enhanced by the alliteration of "petty pace". Alliteration is the repetition of consonant sounds (although it can also mean similarly sounding syllables); assonance is the repetition of vowel sounds. Both alliteration and assonance are powerful tools for controlling rhythm. Overused, they can make the writing appear contrived and flowery, but used appropriately, they are an important part of the writer's tool kit. Take another look at our sample poem,

On the Riprap at Six Mile Beach

The vision of smiles in the holiday throng;
Ripples on a still deep pond.

Note how often sounds are repeated in just three lines and how the repetitions link the words together, helping the mind to form associations: **Rip**rap/**Rip**ples; **Si**x **Mile**/**smile**s; **B**each/d**ee**p; thr**ong**/p**on**d. Notice also the repeated 'i' sounds throughout: R**i**prap, S**i**x, M**i**le, v**i**sion, sm**i**les, **i**n, hol**i**day, R**i**pples, st**i**ll, which bring a consistency of sound to the disparate images.

[*Further reading:* Ezra Pound's *In a Station of the Metro* similarly uses repeated sounds to make connections: Sta**tion**/appari**tion**; M**e**tro/P**e**tals/w**et**; cr**ow**d/b**ou**gh.]

How often assonance and alliteration are used, or whether they are used at all, is part of each individual writer's poetic. If you are writing gritty urban verse, for example, you may decide to concentrate on hard consonant sounds and never use assonance, but if you are writing romantic verse, you may decide to use it frequently. There is no right or wrong, it simply depends on the effect you are trying to achieve.

The sound of language can be used to accentuate the meaning. For example, in the sentence,

"She gave me a hard time."

every word has a hard sound, while in the sentence,

"She soothes me with her voice."

every word has a soft sound. Carefully choosing the sounds of your words can have a great effect on how they are received by the audience.

12

Repetitions

Macbeth's speech also uses repeated words to move the rhythm along, "Tomorrow, and tomorrow, and tomorrow," and "day to day".

[*Further reading:* other examples of poems which use repeated words to drive the rhythm are the section of Christopher Smart's *Jubilato Agno* where every line begins with, 'For...', and *Howl* by Allen Ginsberg in which many lines begin with 'who...' – a rhetorical device called anaphora]

While repetition is used effectively in these works to enhance the rhythm, repeated words are normally something to be avoided. Unless there is a definite reason for repeating words, it is usually best to omit any repetition.

The **wind** stirs
the branches against
the dawn sky.
Seagulls ride the **wind**
over the harbour,
their wing tips brushing
wind-blown clouds.

As you can see here, the repetition of "wind" weakens the poem, the piece is much stronger if "wind" is used only once.

> The **wind** stirs
> the branches against
> the dawn sky.
> Seagulls glide
> over the harbour,
> their wing tips touching
> sun-brushed clouds.

The deciding factor on whether or not to repeat words is if the repetition was accidental or intentional. If a word is repeated just because you happened to use it twice, it is probably best to delete it. If there is something specific you are trying to achieve by repeating a word – for emphasis, or to link back to a previous reference – it may work within the poem. Some poets make it a point never to repeat words, others repeat words often. Whether to use repetition or not is a choice each writer has to make – it is a decision about how to use language and therefore part of the poetic. Repeating or not repeating words demonstrates different ideas about how language can be used to communicate.

Walt Whitman and William Butler Yeats are examples of poets who relied heavily on repeated words as a rhythmical device and as a way of linking lines together. For example, in *The Second Coming*, Yeats purposely repeats the word 'loosed':

> Mere anarchy is **loosed** upon the world,
> The blood-dimmed tide is **loosed**...

and in *Song of Myself*, Whitman uses repeated words throughout:

> I **loaf** and invite my soul,
> I lean and **loaf** at my ease...

T.S. Eliot intentionally repeats words to achieve specific effects. He sometimes repeats words in different contexts to illustrate subtleties of meaning by showing how language allows the same word to be used in wildly different circumstances, for example using 'softly' to describe both the gentle flow of a river and the creeping of a rat. Eliot's repetitions often echo back to a previous usage. For example, in *The Waste Land*, he twice uses 'red' to describe a rock, and later twice uses 'red' to describe some faces in order to establish a connection between the stone and the people. In this way, the repeated words form the basis for a linked pattern of meaning.

But there are other, more subtle kinds of repetition to be aware of:

> The wind awakens
> sleepy branches under
> the dawn sky.
> Seagulls glide
> over the harbour,
> their wing tips touching
> morning clouds.

In this verse, we have the dawn sky and then the morning clouds. The fact that it is early in the day has already been established with "dawn sky", so "morning clouds" seems to be redundant. This kind of repetition, saying the same thing in different ways, is sometimes appropriate, but most often can left out.

13

Overusing Common Parts of Speech

The first line of Macbeth's speech brings out another technique. "To-morrow, and to-morrow, and to-morrow," twice uses the conjunction 'and.' 'And' is a word that links words, ideas and concepts together. As such, it is an effective connecting device. However, it is easily overused. Notice that, while 'and' is used twice in the first line, it does not occur again in the passage. The usage of 'and' needs to be carefully monitored. How often it is used, or if it is used at all, is determined by your poetic.

Sometimes writers will attempt to force an association between two disparate ideas by using 'and' to connect them.

I saw the dawn light over the harbour
and the soft crime of confusion.

As you can see, this is not a very effective technique. It's a good idea to highlight all the 'and's in a poem, then re-read it to see if and where they are necessary. The literary term for the repetition of conjunctions is polysyndeton.

The wind whispers **and** stirs
the branches against the dawn sky
and the seagulls soar
over the harbour,

and their wing tips touch
the low grey clouds.

The verse is much improved by removing the 'and's:

The wind stirs
the branches against the dawn sky.
Seagulls soar
over the harbour,
their wing tips touching
low leaden clouds.

As we saw in the example of *On the Riprap at Six Mile Beach*, the use or exclusion of conjunctions dramatically changes the way language conveys meaning. Some writers use conjunctions heavily, some avoid them at all costs. How conjunctions figure into your writing is part of your poetic. Whether you decide to use conjunctions frequently, sparingly, or not at all will have an effect on the language you use and on the way the meaning of the poem is conveyed to the reader.

Another part of speech to consider is the article. Articles, like conjunctions, are part of the structural element of language. Because of this, their usage or non-usage has a great effect upon a poem. By highlighting the articles, we can decide where they are absolutely necessary.

The wind stirs
the branches against **the** dawn sky.
The seagulls wheel,
crying over **the** harbour,
their wing tips touching
the low lying clouds.

We can see immediately that, in this example, at least a couple of the articles can be removed in the last four lines:

Seagulls wheel,
crying over **the** harbour,
wing tips touching
low lying clouds.

The first two lines present us with other opportunities. We can replace an article with a modifier:

The wind stirs
restless branches against **the** dawn sky.

Or even:

A sombre wind stirs
dead branches against **the** dawn sky.

Or:

The wind scratches
tangled branches against
a pale dawn sky.

In this revision, we have replaced the definite article 'the' with the indefinite article 'a'. Changing the articles avoids repetition, but it is quite different to speak of 'the' wind or 'the' sky than it is to talk of 'a' wind or 'a' sky. Which is the best approach? That depends on your poetic, on what you are trying to achieve. If you are writing in a very direct style, you will probably use more definite articles; if you are writing in a more diffuse style, you might use more indefinite articles.

We can even formulate a poetic in which we dispense with articles altogether for a different effect:

blue wind stirs
black branches under
pink sky

Common parts of speech – prepositions: *of, from, to, in, for, with, on, at*; conjunctions: *and, but, for, like, or, so, yet*; articles: *the, a, an*; adverbs: *just, about*; poly-functional words that fill several grammatical uses or lexical categories: *as, that, than* – are so ubiquitous and expected that we can sometimes read right over them without even noticing they are there.

In poetry, we are working not only with the meanings and sounds of words, but with the structure and syntax of language. The minor parts of speech are the linking and organizing components of language. For example, one of the functions of prepositions is to locate events in space. Prepositions tell us where you are, if you are *at* home, going *to* your home or coming *from* home. While prepositions are necessary, too many 'at's and 'to's can make for dull writing. It's important to look at all the minor parts of speech to see if they are required or if the language can be enlivened by finding creative ways around them through rephrasing.

It is part of the poet's job to be aware of the parts of speech and decide on the appropriate usage. Even poetry that is intentionally written in colloquial language to sound conversational needs an awareness of repeated words and overused common parts of speech.

14

Adjectives, Adverbs and the Pathetic Fallacy

In our last example, "blue wind stirs / black branches under / pink sky," the wind, branches and sky are linked together by colour descriptors; blue, black and pink. When using modifiers, it is important to avoid clichés. Constructions such as, 'sombre wind,' 'restless branches,' and 'pale sky' aren't the most original ways of describing a scene. Our spoken language is riddled with clichés and often we aren't even aware that we are using them, they are rather like the building blocks of everyday communication. Ice cold, blood red, a gentle breeze, a fierce storm, a sad day, a bright smile, light as a feather, sick as a dog, dark as a dungeon are just a few of the common descriptions that fill our conversations. Keeping your adjectives and adverbs exciting can change the way the world is presented in a poem.

Suppose we encountered a poem with the opening lines:

Spring is the callous season,
The dry whisperings of dead of winter
Roused by restless roots
And pale green strivings...

Describing springtime, the time of exuberant growth, renewal and rebirth, as callous is arresting and puts a whole different perspective on our perception of the seasons. With one word, the poem changes the way we view reality. This is how effective use of modifiers can alter the character of a poem.

Adverbs and adjectives are powerful engines of transformation, but they can be dangerous and must be approached with care. Suppose our poem read,

The dry whisperings of winter
Roused by voracious roots
And rapacious green strivings...

The descriptors 'voracious' and 'rapacious' change the character of the piece. We are now giving the reader much more information than conveyed by the milder 'restless' and 'pale'. The piece now seems a little overblown, with the writer telling the reader too much, imposing on the reader instead of suggesting by letting the imagery speak and allowing the reader's own emotions to respond.

Both of these approaches, the subdued and the excessive, have their place in poetry. Each writer has to decide on the use of modifiers appropriate to his or her particular poetic.

[*Further reading:* in the opening line of *The Waste Land*, T.S. Eliot describes the month of April as cruel, providing a new and original point of view on a time usually associated with the joyful awakening of spring.]

Let's look at some examples of how modifiers can affect meanings:

A faltering wind stirs
restless branches...

In this example, the description of the wind as faltering sets the reader up with the expectation that the poem is going to be about hesitation or lack of fulfillment. The wind is faltering, but the branches are restless, which suggests frustration. The participle 'faltering' brings a sense of action to the description, amplified by the restlessness of the branches.

> The heedless, capricious, reckless wind
> snaps at the grey, bare, unprotected branches...

Piling up the descriptors, as in the above excerpt, detracts from the emotional force of the poem rather than helping to build it. Adjectives and adverbs are like shoes for nouns and verbs, providing support and helping them travel farther. If you are going out for a walk, you only need one pair of shoes, taking several pairs with you is superfluous; so don't make your nouns and verbs carry extra baggage, it only weighs them down.

Multiple modifiers can sometimes be used for good effect, but unless you are trying for a specific result, multiple modifiers are best avoided. Excessive use of modifiers often results in work that sounds overwritten.

[*Further reading*: Ted Hughes is a poet who heavily uses modifiers in poems such as *The Thought-Fox*, in which he piles up numerous adjectives to describe the scent of a fox, and *Deaf School*, which uses a series of descriptors, a couple of them compound modifiers, to characterize hard of hearing children.]

Adjectives and adverbs can be used to anthropomorphize nature or attribute human feelings to objects:

> A savage wind stirs
> desperate branches...

The wind is savage, the branches desperate, which implies some kind of emotional struggle. We could also imagine a weary wind, a sultry wind, a mischievous wind, a capricious wind, and many others. Assigning human attributes to inanimate objects is called the 'pathetic fallacy' – 'pathetic' in the sense of feeling, as in sympathetic or empathetic, and not in the sense of contemptible or pitiable. It may also be called personification or anthropomorphism. Some poets shy away from ascribing human traits to natural entities entirely, preferring to keep the physical world inanimate and not imbued with human emotions and/or characteristics. The association of natural elements with human feelings can be a powerful tool, but it can also lead to trite clichés: associating tears with rain, storms with anger, sunshine with happiness, etc.

We regularly use personification in everyday speech, in common phrases such as 'a pitiless sun' or 'a sad day.' Because personifying adjectives are so common, they sometimes creep into poems unawares. It's important to reread poems with an eye to identifying personifying modifiers – and to decide whether you want them there or not. The pathetic fallacy is something that needs to be used sensitively and purposefully.

Pathetic fallacy can be avoided by writing something like,

A frozen wind rattles
ice-bound branches...

in which the modifiers are kept purely physical. The ice-bound branches are consistent with the frozen wind. Notice how the verb has been changed to 'rattles' to suggest the sound the ice covered branches would make. Here, the range of the modifiers is kept quite narrow, within the context of the scene being described. How much you want to restrict your modifiers or let them break outside the context depends on the type of poetry you are writing and the kind of effect you are trying to achieve:

Concrete winds jolt
electric branches...

Whatever approach you take to modifiers, it is important to maintain a consistency of tone. For example, if we wrote:

A joyful wind stirs the branches.
Mournful gulls cry over the harbour.

the adjectives "joyful" and "mournful" give a double message – the reader is likely to be confused over whether your intention is to convey happiness or sadness.

There is another school of thought that says adjectives and adverbs should be used sparingly or not at all, the theory being that if the verbs and nouns are strong enough, they don't need modifiers – let the verbs and nouns do the work.

The wind before the storm
trembles twig and branch

In this example, there are no adjectives or adverbs, the scene is built entirely through description. If modifiers are the shoes of nouns and verbs, sometimes it's nice to kick them off and walk barefoot on the beach. How you decide to use descriptors, conditioners and modifiers is an essential part of your poetic.

15

Proper Usage

One more problematic word to be aware of is 'that'. 'That' can be used in many senses: as a pronoun, as an article or determiner, as an adverb, and as a conjunction. Because of these multiple uses, it creeps into lines in different ways and is often overused. Because it is so invasive, we are sometimes not even aware of using it. Every poem should be reviewed for unnecessary usages of 'that'. "A surging wind jolts/electric branches" is better than "A surging wind that jolts/electric branches..."

Lines can usually be rephrased to remove unnecessary 'that's.

> The wind **that** stirs
> the branches **that** scrape against the sky.
> The gulls **that** glide
> over waves **that** crash on shores
> **that** are hindered with rocks and shoals.

Every usage needs to be carefully reviewed, but there are instances where the use of *that* is appropriate:

> My friend sent me an email **that** said,
> "I love you when your hair's on fire."

although the line could also be rewritten:

> My friend sent me an email to say,
> "I love you when your hair's on fire."

or:

> My friend sent me an email saying,
> "I love you when your hair's on fire."

Which phrasing works best depends on the effect you are trying to achieve. 'That' is often confused with 'which' – they do have slightly different uses grammatically, introducing restrictive and non-restrictive clauses, although in common speech they are frequently interchanged. (As a rule of thumb, 'which' usually follows a comma while 'that' does not.) Getting your grammar right is important, especially if you are submitting poems for publication – you may not know the difference between 'that' and 'which', but you can be darn sure the editor will.

There are a number of similar sounding common words that are often confused, such as its and it's; there, their, and they're; your and you're; to, too and two. If you make basic mistakes in word usage in a submission to a magazine, the editor will pick up on them immediately and possibly dismiss you as an amateur.

It is important to proofread your work for spelling mistakes. Computer spell checkers won't pick up transposition errors such as typing "form" for "from" since "form" is a real word. It takes a human eye to catch all the glitches.

It's fine to experiment with grammar and syntax, but it is important that grammatical innovations be intentional and not accidental. Knowing the parts of speech and their different impacts on the reader will help you to form a poetic that expresses exactly what you want to say. For example, changing the line 'My friend sent me an email that said,' to '...an email to say,' to '...an email saying,' is to change from the past participle, 'said,' to the infinitive, 'to say,' to the present participle, 'saying.' Each form says something slightly different and the verb form you choose will control the nuances of what you are trying to communicate.

16

Line Breaks and Form

Understanding the parts of speech and how they are used will help in translating your thoughts onto the page. For example, suppose you wrote something like this:

My friend sent me an
email that said,
"I love you when
your hair's on fire."

or:

My friend sent me an email to
say, "I love you when your hair's on
fire."

Here we have lines ending with 'an,' 'when,' 'on,' and 'to.' Breaking lines on these minor parts of speech says something about how our language communicates. Check any anthology covering the history of English poetry and see how many poems you can find that have lines ending with articles and prepositions. You won't find many from before the late 20th century. So traditional poets did not end lines with minor parts of speech – why not? What kind of statement does ending a line with a preposition make? It's fine to break lines on unusual parts of speech, the important thing is to understand why you are doing it.

Line breaks generate some interesting questions – and possibilities. Let's look at the line,

"I love you when your hair's on fire."

Presented on one line it comes across as a flat statement. If we break it like this:

"I love you
when your hair's on fire."

the emphasis is put on 'I love you' and the next line, with the conditional phrase 'when your hair's on fire', comes as a surprise. If we put the break after 'when':

"I love you when
your hair's on fire."

the 'when' in the first line tells us that the love is conditional – he doesn't love you all the time, only 'when...' – and so the emphasis is shifted from the first line to the condition in the second line. This is how line breaks can be used to communicate emphasis to the reader.

Another break could be made as:

"I love you when your hair
is on fire."

This break is interesting as it sets up an expectation in the reader and then delivers something unexpected. The 'I love you' conjures up romantic associations such as, "I love you when your hair / catches the morning light" or "when your hair / shimmers with spring rain", so the completion of 'is on fire' is surprising.

There are many schools of thought about line breaks. Some writers think lines should always end with power words, strong nouns and verbs. Other writers rebel against this as old-fashioned and end lines with articles, conjunctions and prepositions. Some think that lines should break at the natural breath pause in the sentence. Others like to break their lines at what they feel are dramatic and surprising moments. Some like to end their lines at punctuation stops, while others never end lines at punctuation stops, preferring to let the lines run one into another, a technique called enjambment. Then again, there are poets who arrange their breaks so that all the lines are of about equal length. The deciding factor is where you want to place the emphasis.

Lines can even be broken in the middle of words:

The wind stirs bare branches un
der a pale sky. Sea
gulls wheel, cry
ing over the harbour,
wing tips tou
ching low morning clouds.

Whatever approach you choose, line breaks should be well thought out and purposeful. They are an important part of your poetic. Where lines are broken says something about your concept of how language is used to communicate. Some writers don't use line breaks at all, letting their lines run on in paragraph style, a form called the prose poem. The prose poem goes back at least as far as Arthur Rimbaud's *Illuminations*, written around 1875.

Related to line breaks are stanza breaks. There is no defining rationale to stanza breaks. Some poets follow regular patterns with each stanza containing the same number of lines: a distich or couplet of two lines, quatrains of four lines, a sestet of six lines, octaves or octets of eight lines, etc. Other poets have irregular stanzas containing different numbers of lines, letting the stanza length be determined by the thought or feeling expressed. Stanzas can end with a full stop or they can be enjambed, breaking in mid-sentence and carrying over into the next. Some poets don't use stanzas at all, writing long poems without any breaks.

Stanza breaks are important to the appearance of the work on the page. The way the poem looks communicates something to the reader and sets up an expectation. A poem with lines of approximately the same length and regular stanzas looks organized and orderly, leading the reader to expect an orderly, contained poem. A poem with lines of unequal length and stanzas with different numbers of lines can appear more free and expressive.

The appearance of the poem can be altered by the placement of the lines on the page. Virtually all rhymed poems and many free verse poems hug the left margin. Breaking away from the left margin, in what is usually called 'open form,' provides a different visual perception of the poem to the reader. Some poets use the spacing and distribution of lines on the page as a form of punctuation, controlling the pauses between phrases with the space between them, by the time it takes the eye to jump from one section to another.

Breaking away from the left margin can also act as a visual expression of the thoughts and feelings contained in the words.

The wind
　　　　stirs
bare　　　branches　　　under
a pale morning sky.

Seagulls
　　　soar
　　over the harbour,
　wing tips brushing
　　　　　low cloud.

The evocative distribution of lines on the page to let the line placement reflect the meaning was experimented with by Stéphane Mallarmé in his poem *Un Coup de Dés* (*A Throw of the Dice*), written shortly before his death in 1898. The abandonment of the left margin was popularized in the mid-20th century by Ezra Pound's *Cantos*, Charles Olson's open form *The Maximus Poems* and by the publication of Lawrence Ferlinghetti's book, *Pictures of the Gone World*.

In the early years of the twentieth century, Mallarmé's work inspired Guillaume Apollinaire to experiment with concrete poetry, in which the form is the content. In his poem *Il Pleut (It's Raining),* Apollinaire spread the letters across the page like raindrops. Since then, concrete poetry has developed into an accepted form and given rise to visual poetry, or vis-po as it is often called, and asemic writing, work which has no semantic content at all.

The important thing to remember with experimental forms is that the content must fit the form; that the form is essential to conveying the meaning of the content – otherwise it will appear to be mere affectation.

17

Simile and Metaphor

Exploring how language is used to communicate is the basis of poetry. However important the content or message of a poem, it needs to be presented in rich, engaging language to be effective. We saw in our first examples, *On the Riprap at Six Mile Beach* and Ezra Pound's *In a Station of the Metro*, how language can still communicate effectively even when the connecting words, the conjunctions, are removed.

The conjunctions 'like' and 'as' are used in comparative constructions called similes. "She went **as** red **as** a beet," "He ran **like** a rabbit." Simile is a type of metaphor, an association between similar qualities of two things. The difference is that while simile is a comparison – one thing resembles another – metaphor is an identification: one thing has the qualities of another. A metaphor defines one thing in terms of another.

'Hard as a rock' and 'cold as ice' are similes. A simile can be turned into a metaphor by using the comparative as an adjective or adverb, as in 'rock hard' or 'ice cold.' To say,

'Hatred is like a rabid dog,' is a simile.
'Hatred is a rabid dog,' is a metaphor.
'The rabid dog of hatred,' is also a metaphor.

Metaphor is one of our basic means of communication. There are so many things that can't be conveyed to another person without some kind of comparison. No one else can experience our inner emotional states, so the only way we can tell others how we feel is through an association with something that others can identify with. "He's as sad as a beached whale." "She's as happy as a field of spring flowers."

How metaphor is used is one of the defining features of a poetic. The more original the comparison, the more it will engage the reader, such as Byron's "She walks in beauty, like the night..." or William Wordsworth's "I wandered lonely as a cloud..." In the early 20th century, the Modernists, under the influence of French Symbolism and Surrealism, began to make more unusual comparisons:

Morning sprawls across the horizon
Like a body on a mortuary slab.

[*Further reading:* In *The Love Song of J. Alfred Prufrock*, T.S. Eliot uses an arresting simile comparing the evening to a sedated patient. Eliot was much influenced by the French poetry of the time, especially Jules Laforgue and possibly Comte de Lautréamont, among others.]

Championed by the Modernists, striking comparisons were adopted by mainstream poets, particularly the Confessional poets of the mid-twentieth century. In the poem *Oedipus Resurrected* we find the simile, "Cicadas...dream...like...temples." But the writer doesn't state this straight out, he intentionally interrupts the construction to stretch out the metaphor, thereby increasing the drama by making the reader wait for the expected completion. The full two lines read:

When cicadas, locked in closed-wing slumber, dream
down the frost
Like heuristic temples, and the trees are ice.

[*Further reading:* Sylvia Plath is a poet known for her original similes. In her poem *Electra on Azalea Path* she indirectly compares sleeping bees to stones. The simile is drawn out over a couple of lines for dramatic effect.]

Some writers use metaphor very little or not at all.

The wind stirs
bare branches under
a pale sky.
Seagulls soar
over the harbour,
wing tips touching
low morning cloud.

This verse is purely descriptive, relying on direct reporting and avoiding any comparisons. Other writers use metaphor and simile extensively.

The writhing serpent of the wind
worries lace branches
under a pale porcelain sky.
A lone gull draped in grey mourning
glides over water blue as tears,
the pen tips of its arcing wings
scribing messages of sorrow
on the obdurate clouds.

Overuse of metaphor can result in a piece being overwritten and detract from a poem rather than enhancing it. There is also the danger of mixing metaphors. In the example above, the wind is compared to a writhing snake that worries the branches, but worrying something is the action of a dog, so the characteristics of two different creatures, a snake and a dog, are mixed together.

18

Imagery

Closely related to metaphor, and often serving as the foundation for metaphor, is the image. An image is a visual representation of something else. A picture of a tree is not a tree, it is a representation of a tree. Images usually represent objects in the physical world, although we can create images from imagination. In literature, an image is a picture drawn with words.

Our little sample poem:

The wind stirs
bare branches under
a pale sky.
Seagulls soar
over the harbour,
wing tips brushing
low morning cloud.

is an image, it paints a picture of a harbour at dawn. Images can be stark and spare or lively and colourful – and everything in between. Images can be used to set a scene, establish a location, generate atmosphere or express emotion.

Images are not confined to representing what they depict. An image of a lone gull circling a deserted harbour may suggest feelings of emptiness and longing. It is this connection between the subject described and human emotion, between our outer and inner worlds, which makes images so powerful.

The difference between image and metaphor is that in a metaphor both a subject and a comparator are named, while the image stands alone. For example, if we were to say,

My soul is aflame like a fiery furnace...

we are using a simile to compare the soul to a fiery furnace. If we were to say,

In the fiery furnace of my soul...

we are using a metaphor, stating that the soul is a fiery furnace. In the metaphor, both the soul and the furnace are identified. But if we say,

A fiery furnace burns within
Consuming both remorse and sin.

we are presenting the image of the furnace only; the soul is not mentioned, merely implied. Because the comparator is not named, the associative effect of images can be much broader than the more specific and restricted metaphor. Images allow language to speak beyond itself.

In a poem such as *Lost Rain* we find a description of a dream journey through a nightmare landscape which concludes:

where the road ends
in an empty field
and the stars go out.

There is no further explanation, no clarification; the poet lets the image speak for itself. It is obvious that the poem is about more than a dream of coming to the end of the road; the image is used to describe some inner turmoil. The poet is speaking beyond the description.

[*Further reading:* In *The Far Field,* Theodore Roethke similarly uses an image of a car spinning its wheels in a snowbank until the engine dies and the lights fade as the battery fails. Roethke doesn't add any explanatory information, he allows the image to evoke a feeling in the reader – the reader is taken past the literal meaning of the words.]

This ability of images to speak beyond the language was emphasized in the early 20th century by Ezra Pound, one of the founders of a poetic movement called Imagism. Influenced by oriental forms, it was a style of poetry firmly grounded in the sensual image, devoid of emotive modifiers or contextual markers. Later in the century, Deep Image poetry was developed by Robert Bly and others. Deep Image poetry was more narrative than that of the original Imagists, owing much to the surrealist-influenced imagery of Federico Garcia Lorca and other Spanish and South American writers.

Images do not have to be factual; elements can be mixed together to expand the scope of the image. Consider:

> Within twisted nerves
> eagles haunt the winds
> of muted impulse

Realistically, it is impossible for there to be eagles inside someone's nerves, but the poet combines the image elements to provide an impression of a state of being that could not be described by sticking to the bare facts. It is characteristic of image-based poetry that the poem does not begin, "I feel like there are eagles in my nerves," the poet leaves out all reference to himself or his feelings and lets the image do the talking. The intent of the image is to stir within the reader the same kinds of sensations that the writer is experiencing, something that couldn't be said in ordinary plain language.

[*Further reading:* Robert Bly's poem *Waking from Sleep* uses the image of seagulls riding the blood-breeze inside a vein. Of course, no one can really have gulls inside their veins, but Bly is describing a state in which emotion is felt in the physical body, a condition that everyday language is too limited to express.]

This is what images do: they allow us to connect our feelings with someone else's through the web of the image. If someone ordered you to "Feel sad!" it probably wouldn't make you feel sad. But if you were confronted by an image of a magnificent tiger pacing in a tiny cage, it may well stir up feelings of sadness, and move beyond mere sadness to feelings of frustration and yearning for freedom.

It's fascinating to browse through an anthology of poetry and see the various ways in which different writers use imagery. Some let the images stand alone; some interweave images into a larger narrative; some use them as short, sharp stabs of insight; some use images in cascades of disconnected sensory phenomena; some use an image to capture a fleeting moment; and some even add explanations to their imagery, as in this poem:

Old Brown Shoes

everything turns
on

the old brown
shoes

splashed with sun
light

on the green porch
steps

Here the writer does not simply present the image of old shoes on the porch steps so we can infer the importance of their place in the scheme of things, but tells us that the state of the world rests upon them: he wants to make sure we understand that this is not a poem about a pair of shoes, but about the order of the universe and the way we structure reality.

[*Further reading:* William Carlos Williams uses the same ploy in *The Red Wheelbarrow*. Williams doesn't trust that the image by itself will communicate his intent, so he tells us how much is dependent on the wheelbarrow in its idyllic setting.]

Imagery opens up a vast and exciting world. Poetic imagery can be implemented in an infinite variety of ways. How you use imagery is based in your basic concept of how language communicates. In our examples, Theodore Roethke used direct description to create an evocative image; Robert Bly concocted a bizarre image to communicate something that normal description was incapable of expressing; William Carlos Williams felt that the image alone was not enough to convey what he meant and that a helpful explanation was needed to steer the reader in the right direction.

These represent three different theories of how language can convey meaning – three different poetics. It is your theory of language, your poetic, which will determine the appropriate use of imagery in your own work.

19

Editorializing and Message Poems

Editorializing occurs in a poem when the writer explains what the poem is about rather than letting the writing speak for itself.

> The lonely wind stirs
> sorrowful branches against
> an empty dawn sky.
> I feel so sad.
> A solitary seagull flaps
> forlornly over the desolate harbour,
> wing tips brushing
> aching clouds,
> yearning to be free.

This writer is constantly telling the reader what feelings are being imparted by using emotionally descriptive words such as 'lonely' and 'sorrowful', and interpolating statements like 'I feel so sad.' The writer is declaring that there is something distressful here rather than evoking the feeling through the writing. Most writers choose to avoid telling the reader what to feel, allowing the emotion to be expressed through the language; it is much more effective to think up a scene or situation or image which suggests the feelings you want to convey rather than relying on explication.

Editorializing sometimes devolves into preaching. This is especially true of message poems, poems on themes of injustice, politics, inhumanity and environmental issues. These poems are often more polemic than poetry with the message overshadowing the writing. There's nothing wrong with writing on hot issues, but remember that you are writing a poem that delivers a message, not a message in the form of a poem.

Personal poetry often suffers from overwriting. The poet is so desperate to be understood and get the point across that the poetry is sacrificed to the content. You may have deep and intense feelings, but simply smearing them across the page will probably not result in poetry. Deep and intense feelings need to be expressed in equally deep and intense language.

20

Punctuation

Another element of a poetic is punctuation. Whether you use punctuation or not depends on the kind of poetry you are writing. There are poets who mix their punctuation, putting in some commas and periods and leaving out others – this is generally not good practice. The rule of thumb about punctuation is: be consistent – either use it correctly or leave it out entirely. Some writers use line breaks or spacing in place of punctuation, breaking the line or adding spaces where a comma or period would normally occur.

How you use punctuation makes a statement about how language communicates. If you write with punctuation you are saying that the formal structure of language is important to convey your meaning. If you write without punctuation you are implying that you do not want to control the reader; that the reader can be freed from being told when to pause and stop. Or you may be demonstrating that the reader can be directed where to pause or stop by means other than conventional punctuation – which means that language can be used to communicate in ways beyond the predictable.

21

Effective Openings

Before you can use any of these devices and techniques and put your poetic into action, you have to start your poem. Where to begin? This is a difficult problem and your creative solutions will help to develop your writing talent. Many writers start with an arresting first line that hooks the reader in. T.S. Eliot does this with the opening line of *The Waste Land*, in which the month of April is described as cruel, and we saw it in our example, "Spring is the callous season," – the reader wants to know why the narrator thinks Spring is callous and will read on to find out.

[*Further reading:* The hook technique is used by Allen Ginsberg in the opening line of his long poem *Howl*, in which he states that the finest intellects of his times were ruined by insanity, left hungry frantic alone.

The line raises a lot of questions in the reader's mind which need answering – who were these extraordinary people and how did they come to be ruined by insanity? Both Eliot and Ginsberg start their poems with challenging statements that engage the reader's interest.

Allen Ginsberg uses another interesting technique in the first line of *Howl*: omitting the commas that would normally separate the descriptive words to purposely run the words together, creating a sense of urgency, rushing the reader on to the next line.]

While Eliot and Ginsberg raise questions through controversial statements, John Keats starts his poem *La Belle Dame sans Merci* with a question:

O what can ail thee, Knight at arms
Alone and palely loitering?

Here a question is posed and the reader is led to expect some kind of answer.

[*Further reading:* Stevie Smith begins her poem *Pretty* with a question, asking why 'pretty' is held in such low esteem. Stevie Smith doesn't follow this question up with an essay type response – "Pretty is underrated because..." – but rather takes the reader on a journey illustrated with images and situations to demonstrate new and unusual perspectives on the concept of pretty.]

Another approach is to plunge the reader into the middle of a situation, as in this example:

Avoiding the fluorescent agony of empty malls
and the lonesome lights beyond the desolate yards

Starting the first line with the active present participle 'Avoiding' immediately involves the reader in the action of the poem. Notice also how the reader is drawn along with repeated 'O' sounds in Avoiding, fluorescent, agony, of, lonesome, beyond, desolate; and the 'L' sounds in fluorescent, malls, lonesome, lights, desolate. The poet also invokes the pathetic fallacy by using the disturbing term 'agony' in association with the empty malls and employing the emotionally-charged adjective 'lonesome' to describe the distant lights rather than a more objective descriptor, such as 'remote' or 'isolated.'

'Avoiding' coupled with 'agony' and 'lonesome' creates an impression of separation and alienation; the reader feels the tension and wants to know the reason for the poet's estrangement and how it will be resolved. The poem is set near 'empty malls' and 'desolate yards' rather than in a populated area, images that emphasize the feelings of disconnection and dislocation.

In these two lines, the writer uses four distinct techniques to capture attention: pulling the reader into the situation with the use of the present participle 'Avoiding'; utilizing assonance and alliteration in the repeated 'O' and 'L' sounds to move the reader through the lines; using imagery and the pathetic fallacy to evoke emotional tension; and, finally, creating a need for the resolution of the disconcerting emotional state of loneliness and isolation. The important thing to remember is that this was not accidental; the poet used these devices on purpose, he deliberately constructed his opening to employ these techniques as ways of engaging the reader.

[*Further reading:* an example of an opening using multiple stratagems to draw the reader in is *The Strand at Lough Beg* by Seamus Heaney. In just the first two lines, Heaney grabs the audience in several ways: involving the reader with the use of a present participle; utilizing alliteration in repeated 'L' sounds; using imagery and the pathetic fallacy for emotional effect; and invoking uncomfortable feelings of sadness and loss which the reader feels a need to resolve.]

Unusual use of language can entice a reader to continue on. In the E.E. Cummings poem entitled, *the Cambridge ladies who live in furnished souls*, the reader is arrested by something strange – instead of the ordinary and expected 'furnished rooms', the reader is confronted by the state of the ladies' souls. The reader will want to find why these ladies live in such odd circumstances, and see what other strange things they may get up to.

E.E. Cummings used the first line of *the Cambridge ladies who live in furnished souls* as the title. This can sometimes be an effective way of placing the reader right in the middle of things, as in this example,

Here Is My Picture:

taken long ago.
It appears on first glance
to be blurred

but that is merely a compulsion
of my vagueness

This poet doesn't waste any time involving the reader. The first line is the title, *Here Is My Picture*; the next line, 'taken long ago' follows directly from the title, so by the time the reader starts into the body of the poem, the associative links are already established and the attention is already engaged. The title forms an immediate bond between the narrator and the reader, as if someone were handing a picture to a friend saying, "Here's a picture of me..." The narrator is giving something to the reader.

The title and first line are flat statements that put the reader in the frame: the reader knows that we are dealing with an old photograph of the narrator; which raises the question, what is so special about this picture that someone would want to write a poem about it? The reader is invited to explore this question with the second line beginning, 'It appears on first glance...', which implies that things are not as they may initially seem and we need to examine the photograph closely in order to discern what is really going on. In this way, the poet sets up an expectation in the reader: that something hidden will be revealed.

To capture the reader's interest in the first few lines is quite a challenge. Sometimes in the process of composing a poem, the writer will take some time to come to what the poem is really about. It is often necessary to go back and cut away all the extraneous material. It is easy to imagine another writer beginning the poem with:

In a secluded cabin beside a still lake, forgotten
at the back of a neglected drawer
in a dusty bureau, there lies
a blurry picture of me
taken long ago…

The poet avoids all this atmospheric scene-setting because she knows that what is important in the poem is the old picture and what it reveals. At the beginning of this poem the setting is not relevant; the writer presents only what the reader needs to know.

[*Further reading:* Margaret Atwood's *This Is a Photograph of Me:* is an example of a poem in which the title serves as the first line.]

The key to devising effective openings is asking the questions, "What does the reader need to know?" and "How do the first lines draw the reader in?" The answer to these questions depends in large part on the way you use language, on the elements of your poetic. What the reader needs to know depends on the focus of the poem. Each approach requires a different way of using language, which means a different poetic.

22

Effective Endings

Eventually you will come to what is often the most difficult part of the poem: the ending. What is the best way to effectively end a poem? There are many approaches to effective endings; which ones you choose to use depends on what you feel is appropriate for the type of poetry you are writing.

One approach is to end a poem with a final summing up, bringing the narrative to a definite conclusion. For example,

> In the end he will return
> to find only what he left behind.

[*Further reading:* Michael Ondaatje ends his long poem *Burning Hills* with a concluding summation.]

Another approach is to leave the reader with a final insight or epiphany:

> Love does not always
> end in peace.

[*Further reading:* Charles Olson adds an insightful ending to *Le Bonheur, part 1 of Variations Done for Gerald Van De Wiele.*]

Sometimes epiphanic, punch-line endings can surprise and shock the reader, as in the final line of *Oedipus*

Resurrected, a poem about a young man coming to terms with the loss of his father:

My happiness was our doom, my love our death.

Startling endings can turn the reader's world on its head, as in:

I burn memories like water.

[*Further reading:* Sylvia Plath is known for her surprising and enigmatic closing lines. Examples can be found in *Electra on Azalea Path* and *Lady Lazarus.*]

Some poems end with a reference back to the opening lines, as in this piece beginning:

First light brought the promise of completion

and ending 25 lines later with:

As he knew when he saw light first.

[*Further reading:* Richard Wilbur ties the first and last lines together in *First Snow in Alsace.*]

Many modern poems are open ended, concluding with a matter-of-fact statement that relates to the rest of the poem, but avoids any definite wrapping-up. The poem here is not a self-contained unit, but something that connects to the wider world.

The wind does not cease
but sings across the ocean
to the farthest shore

[*Further reading:* an example of a poem with an open ending is Gary Snyder's *Mid-August at Sourdough Mountain Lookout.*]

If a poem can start with a question, as we saw in Keat's *La Belle Dame sans Merci* and Stevie Smith's *Pretty*, it can also end with a question, as in *Curtain Fall*, a poem about modern theatre:

in the end
we are left
with nothing
but a question –

or is it
an answer?

[*Further reading:* Langston Hughes ends his poem *Harlem* with a question.]

There are, of course, many other ways to end poems and you will probably want to try several different approaches to your endings to avoid becoming clichéd and repetitious. Variety keeps poetry interesting.

23

Structuring a Poem

What is the best way to structure a poem? There is no straight answer to that question. The structure of a poem depends on many elements: the opening, the ending, the content, whether the piece is narrative or non-linear, etc. Basically, the structure of each poem is unique and is designed to bring out the theme or intent of the work. There are some techniques and devices we can use in structuring and some things to keep in mind.

We want to maintain the reader's interest between the opening and the ending. A poem may have a startling first line, but if it is followed by droning filler, no one is going to continue reading right through to the end. Everything in the poem must have a purpose, it must be there for a reason.

Most poems are designed with some kind of build in anticipation or expectation, increasing the tension towards a climax or crescendo. The ending can either be a resolution, releasing the tension; or a dramatic summing up which leaves the reader with the tension; or even a denial or reversal of the tension.

Here is a poem dealing with the moment of hearing about the death of jazz musician Charlie Parker, known as Bird:

The Night Bird Died

Saturday March 12th 1955 in a Barrow Street dive
taking a break after looking for *Master Takes*
and other lost jazz records
as a birthday present for Jackie
finding nothing but honky-tonk blues
finally settling on Gillespie and Monk
then getting my shoes shined and buying a paper
from the newsstand on 7th Avenue
and forgetting to pick up a copy of *Downbeat*
for Chick like I had promised
and grooving to the blow of a cool quartet
until the news came on
and the radio sucked all the air from the room.
A horn sounded in the street, then fell silent.

This whole poem is really a set-up for the ending. The writer's skill comes in deciding how much material is needed to bring the reader to the point where the shock of the ending is felt. If the writer had gone on listing the places he went and the things he did, he would have been in danger of drowning the audience in unnecessary trivia and risk losing the reader's interest. On the other hand, too little of the atmospheric scene building would have diminished the disorienting effect of the ending. That is the delicate balance: enough material to direct readers where you want them to go, but not so much that they get lost on the journey.

This poem is about the jazz world and incorporates many jazz references. The first twelve lines are one long sentence using minimal punctuation to capture the run-on urgency of bebop jazz. The last line, following a full stop, is like the coda to a piece of music. The informal, improvisational language reflects the spontaneity of a jazz solo. The piece is constructed like a jazz session – an attempt to have the form complement the content.

[*Further reading: The Day Lady Died* by Frank O'Hara is an example of a poem in which the body of the poem is scene-building for the dramatic ending. O'Hara begins with a specific date and time, then continues with an account of his day busily running errands until he is stopped by the news of the death of Billie Holiday.]

Of course, there are poems in which it is the journey itself that is important, not the ending. These are usually longer poems such as T.S. Eliot's *The Waste Land*, Allen Ginsberg's *Howl* or Ezra Pound's *Cantos*, works which have inconclusive endings. The poem as process rather than statement is an important concept in much Post-Modern work, although the pull of the forceful closing line is strong and you will find many intentionally non-linear Post-Modern poems ending with a final kick.

[*Further reading:* Language poet Bob Perelman concludes his poem *China* with a straight admonition to the reader.]

To sustain the reader's interest you need something to say and an interesting way of saying it. Language can be made engaging through the rhetorical techniques we have covered: simile and metaphor, images, dramatic verbs, insightful descriptions, arresting modifiers, expressive line breaks, rhythmical variations and so on.

It is in the structure of the poem where we can really display our poetic and show our own concept of how language communicates meaning. In our little sample poem:

The wind stirs
bare branches under
a pale morning sky.
Seagulls soar
over the harbour.
Wing tips brush
low cloud.

we have three sentences. How are they connected? The common, surface understanding might be that they form a normal unified description of a scene. But suppose each unit is distinct and from a different setting. The wind in the trees could be a memory from childhood, the wings in the clouds could be imagination or an expectation for the future.

> *childhood:*
> The wind in the trees.
> *today:*
> Seagulls over the harbour.
> *tomorrow:*
> Wing tips in cloud.

The addition of the time element dramatically changes the meaning of the poem. The insertion of 'childhood' shifts the poem from the objective, about a harbour scene, to the subjective, about the narrator's life. It also shifts the images from descriptive to figurative: the 'wind in the trees' isn't a description of what the writer sees, but a metaphorical image representing the writer's childhood. We could have written,

> My childhood was like the wind in the trees.
> Today is like seagulls over the harbour.
> Tomorrow will be like wing tips in cloud.

As you can see, this rendition uses the conjunction 'like.' Omitting the conjunction alters the normal, syntactical, descriptive similes by changing them to disjunctive images.

What these three versions demonstrate are different concepts of how language communicates meaning. The first example is objective, descriptive and syntactical. This writer thinks that the intent of the poem is best conveyed in a description using straight-forward conventional language.

The second example is subjective, figurative and disjunctive. This writer feels that the intent of the poem is best conveyed through metaphor, personal images and by breaking down the reader's expectations of continuity through the use of time disruption and disjunctive language.

The third example is a combination of the first two, using objective language in a subjective sense.

The first writer uses modifiers and colourful verbs to accentuate the scene: bare branches, pale sky, soaring birds and brushing wings. The second writer has stripped away all the descriptors and presented flat statements. This is a very different use of language and a very different understanding of how to communicate, of what is necessary for the reader to perceive the intent of the poem. The third writer is muddled, unsure of what is being said or how to say it – which shows how important it is to have an idea of what you want to write before you put down the first word; if you don't know what you are doing, the reader won't know what you are doing either.

These examples illustrate how the poetic is embodied in the very text of the poem. Small changes were made to the structure of the sample poem, but the effect on the meaning is profound. Radical alteration of the structure radically alters the author's statement and the reader's perception:

wind
        (stir soar brush)
branches bare
    harbour   cloud
sky   wing tips
gulls morning
   over pale
low   (stir soar brush)

This arrangement raises a number of questions. The verbs are all grouped together and separated from the nouns and adjectives by brackets. There are no articles or conjunctions. There are no capital letters and no punctuation. The words are all jumbled up, not in their normal order, making the poem deliberately unstructured. What is this writer trying to say? We saw in Lewis Carroll's *Jabberwocky* that meaning could be conveyed by sentence structure in the absence of normal words; here we have an example of meaning being conveyed by words in the absence of normal language structure.

How far can language be stretched and still convey meaning? Does a poem even have to have a meaning? Does a meaningless existence generate meaningless poems? There is a catch here: a meaningless poem is making a statement that a poem does not necessarily have to have a meaning – and in making such a statement it actually does have a meaning. The poem itself may be nonsense, but there is purpose in the concept of the work, the nonsense was written for a reason – even if the reason is a negative one to deconstruct the obvious, it is still a reason. The nonsensical becomes meaningful.

24

Inspiration and Content

Where does inspiration come from and how can we find it? Basically, inspiration comes from unresolved tensions. As human beings, we are always trying to find solutions to life's imperfections; we are always seeking completion. If a baby is crying, our instinctual response is to care for it and take away the discomfort. If we sing the scale do-re-me-fa-so-la-ti- we can't stop until we have resolved the tension with the final -do! Emotionally, philosophically, politically, spiritually we are always trying to figure things out, to know the best way to respond, to act, to feel, to think, to be. Within ourselves we may feel mixed-up, unsure of who we are and our place in the world. These uncertainties inside ourselves and between our inner selves and the outside world create tensions that are constantly seeking resolution.

In our subconscious minds we have a world view: a set of ideas that form our basic understanding of how the world works. We may believe that love conquers all; that good will be rewarded and evil punished; that money can't buy happiness; that there is some good in everyone; that truth is better than lies; that justice will prevail; and many similar common concepts. This set of ideas is constantly being either confirmed by or challenged by the physical circumstances in which we find ourselves. The frictions between expectation and reality are the source of our existential angst.

It is from these tensions that inspiration is born. Our job as writers is to devise a language that expresses the anxiety. The expression of the tension is more important than the resolution, for the stress doesn't always have to be reconciled. Here is an example of prolonged unease:

The dance of death will not be stilled.
Though the music may change
The gavotte goes on –
Pirouette, arabesque, tango, waltz,
Mad whirling and jive jumping
To the ceaseless throb within.

In this case, the thrust of the poem is not in the relieving the pressure, but in sustaining the tension.

[*Further reading:* In his *Sonnet 23*, John Berryman writes of his inner emotional turmoil. At the end of the poem, the unrest is not transformed into sweet rest, but continues to quake within him.

In *Wall Mending*, Robert Frost starts out with a direct statement about how the world works, telling us how Nature despises walls. This sets up an inspiring tension between the act of mending walls and the forces which try to bring them down. A neighbour resolves this tension with a counter-statement about how relationships between neighbours depend on the strength of their walls. But the narrator finds this answer unsatisfactory, being of the opinion that the neighbour is in the dark about how things really are. So now we have two tensions: between the wall and the natural inclination of things to fall down, and between the narrator and the neighbour. Neither of these tensions are resolved; the poem ends with the neighbour simply repeating the catch-all folksy wisdom about strong walls. The force of the poem comes from the feeling that there will never be any solution.]

Many poems do end with a resolution of the tension. Dylan Thomas' *A Refusal to Mourn the Death, by Fire, of a Child in London* concludes with the uncompromising statement, "After the first death, there is no other." – a line as final and forceful as the closing chord of a symphony, leaving no room for argument or discussion.

Even a positive poem, such as Robert Browning's *Pippa Passes*, which ends with the upbeat statement, "All's right with the world!" creates tension, for it suggests that there are times when everything is not right with the world and that the peaceful beauty of the spring morning is but a rare, fleeting moment, not a constant state.

Another poet faced with Browning's inspiring spring day may be disturbed by the contrast of the seeming tranquility of nature and the violent turbulence of life. Yet another may be reminded of past times spent in similar surroundings with a lost love and be consumed with feelings of sadness and remorse. Another may become angry at how nature is being destroyed by pollution and rampant development. There are as many reactions to the scene as there are people, but each response depends upon the interplay of subjective expectations (that is, our inner understanding of the way we think or feel the world should work) and objective experience.

Often, we are not aware of what our basic beliefs are until they are disturbed by events beyond our control. We may feel that we are in control of our lives until something unexpected occurs – a car accident, a hurricane, an earthquake, someone with a different ethnicity or religion moving in next door – and shows us that we were living an illusion, that our lives can be turned upside down by random, inexplicable forces in a moment.

Are we masters of our fate or are we victims of circumstance? Are we essentially free spirits or are we prisoners in a violent universe? Is there a divine presence watching over us, or does it all come down to dumb luck? Does everything have a purpose or is existence random and absurd? Is love a positive or a destructive emotion? Such existential questions about our state of being, of the human condition, underlie all our thoughts, our dreams, our actions, our work.

Themes such as these may not overtly appear in a poem, but they will form the foundation for whatever is built over them and will determine the kinds of poems that are written. Someone who believes that true love is eternal would never write a poem like W.H. Auden's *As I Walked Out One Evening* in which the city clocks tell the lover that Time cannot be overcome and that everything passes away in dismal futility.

Our fundamental attitudes form the basis of the way we will react to the situations in which we find ourselves. Our reactions are the basis of our poems. Even intensely personal poetry is about how the sense of self is impinged upon by the world. Inspiration is being open to the challenges of life.

Many writers find inspiration through their ability to present a view of reality which allows their readers to see the world and their place in it in a new context. Stevie Smith, in her poem *Not Waving but Drowning*, writes of mistaken signals – what appears to be a normal gesture is really a desperate cry for help.

The technique of building tension between two different perceptions of the world is exploited by Matthew Arnold in *Dover Beach* where, into the calm of a moonlit night, is introduced "The eternal note of sadness." The world is not as it appears, for though it seems beautiful, it "Hath really neither joy, nor love, nor light." In a similar reversal, Thomas Hardy creates tension by introducing the unexpected in *The Darkling Thrush* – on hearing a bird's song he finds ecstatic hope hidden in a desolate winter's day. Carl Sandburg twists the view of *Chicago* as a wicked, crooked, brutal place into that of a hard-working, energetic city continually raising up, tearing down, rising again – a place swelled with pride and rocking with raucous laughter – to develop the tension between the two opposing points of view.

A great deal of poetry takes its inspiration from finding a way of relating the particular to the whole. Examples of this can be found in Wordsworth's *Lines Composed a Few Miles Above Tintern Abbey*, which begins as an inner reflection on memories and develops into general principles about our relationship to the natural world, such as, "Nature never did betray / the heart that loved..."; or in Allen Ginsberg's *America* which starts with some very specific facts – the date and the exact amount of change in his pocket – then expands into an exposition of inequality and injustice in American society; and, of course, William Blake's oft quoted *Auguries of Innocence*: "To see the world in a grain of sand...And eternity in an hour."

Besides this unique point of view, we need the language to articulate it. The kind of language we use will complement the kinds of things we write about. For example, in *The Waste Land*, T.S. Eliot uses fragmented images and language to mirror the fragmented state of the world after the First World War. He was concerned about the loss of culture and so wrote of a damaged world vulgarized and debased by popular songs and common tastes. Through the use of unconventional language, Eliot was able to draw others into his dyspeptic view of the world.

25

Objective / Subjective

One final, but important, area to address is the point of view. Take a look at your work and see how many subjective 'I' poems you have. If all your poems are 'I' poems, you may want to consider broadening your range. We all start out writing about ourselves, but it is an important step to begin writing about life and the world in general rather than concentrating solely on ourselves, our experiences and our personal emotional turmoil.

In the late 20th century era of Post-Modernism, the emphasis was on objective poetry and personal poetry became virtually taboo. However, the early 21st century has witnessed an explosion of personal poetry. Personal poetry needs to be approached carefully to avoid coming across as self-absorbed – too much self-involvement makes it difficult for the reader to access the intensity. All of us have written about our inner anguish, but unless we have deep and varied feelings communicated in unique and engaging ways, we end up saying the same things as hundreds of other poets; after a while it just starts to sound like self-indulgent me-me-me-me.

Whether you write subjectively, about your inner states, or objectively, about the world around you, is basic to your approach to poetry and language. Some poets write exclusively in the subjective mode and others are exclusively objective. Most writers work with both points of view, having a mix of subjective and objective material.

Intensely personal autobiographical poetry, called Confessional Poetry, became popular in the mid-20th century, partly as a reaction to the relentless objectivity of the Modernists in the earlier part of the century. Even the Confessional poets, however, didn't simply write out their feelings, they translated their trauma through the techniques of their poetic. They avoided sentimentality and self-pity through the use of highly figurative and metaphorical, almost mythic, language, as in *Oedipus Resurrected*:

> I am the fable of an enigmatic patricide,
> my blue lips hold the rusted secret of my mutilation

[*Further reading*: Sylvia Plath is a Confessional poet who transformed her inner conflicts through metaphorical, mythic language. An example is her poem *Electra on Azalea Path*.]

In the writing of Chilean poet Pablo Neruda, an 'I' appears in a great deal of his poetry, but it is clear that the 'I' refers to something much larger than the poet's persona, it is a social conscience, the collective 'I' of our shared humanity offering love in the face of injustice and oppression.

Always remember that you are not writing just for yourself, you are writing for an audience. Poetry is more than sincerity and honesty in reporting personal feelings. It is about relating those feelings to a larger world, whether that world be emotional, physical, experiential, psychological, intellectual, spiritual, imagined, social or political. It is about putting your thoughts and feelings into the context of our shared reality so that the reader can benefit from your insight.

Sometimes the 'I' is an unnecessary intrusion into the poem and can be cut.

The wind stirs
the branches against
the dawn sky.
I hear the seagulls crying
over the harbour,
their wing tips brushing
lowering grey clouds.

The "I hear" doesn't really need to be there. It makes for a stronger line to simply present an image of the gulls; the sudden interruption of the 'I' disrupts the flow of the imagery.

The wind stirs
the branches against
the dawn sky.
The seagulls wheel, crying
over the harbour,
their wing tips brushing
lowering grey clouds.

It's important to re-read 'I' poems, to figure out what they are really about and decide if the 'I' is absolutely necessary or not. As a rule of thumb, if the emotion you want to communicate is contained within the images, leave the 'I' out.

The same interruption that happens with 'I' also occurs with the sudden introduction of an unidentified 'you' into a poem.

An inconstant wind whisks
across the dawn sky.
You went away
without a word.
I watch the gulls circle
over fragile cliffs.

The reader is going to wonder just who is this 'you'? Is this poem addressed to the reader? Or to some specific, unnamed person? To a lover or a parent or a child or a friend or a dead relative? Or is 'you' used in a universal sense of people in general? The writer knows to whom the poem is addressed so why keep it a secret from the reader? Poetry is more than private communication.

The problem can be addressed simply by changing the 'you' to an identifier such as 'my love,' thus distinguishing the object of the poem for reader:

An inconstant wind whisks
the dawn sky.
My love went away
without a word.

Unnecessary 'I's and 'you's, as well as other undefined pronouns such as 'we', 'us', 'they' etc., occur frequently in the work of beginning poets as they are such natural and common parts of our everyday speech – cleaning them up is part of the process of revising and polishing a poem.

The problem with undefined pronouns can be seen in this excerpt:

Dreaming After Dreams

The bed that once held your dreams
is torn away.
The love taken from you
will be restored
in time.

These words are obviously intended to comfort someone, but who? The poem resonates differently whether it is taken as addressed to an ex-lover, a friend with a broken heart, a bereaved parent, the widow of a soldier killed in a war, or to the reader whom the writer assumes has suffered some heartache – each reading has a different emotional impact and the audience is left guessing exactly what the writer means. *Dreaming After Dreams* could have been inspired by a cat that had to be given away to a new home, but how would the reader know that? Leaving the 'you' undefined is rarely the best approach.

[*Further reading:* You may occasionally find works by accomplished writers addressed to an undefined 'you.' For example, Derek Walcott's poem *Love After Love* speaks to an unidentified someone, but even here the message has a different meaning depending on who the reader assumes the words are intended for. It is an illuminating exercise to read poems like this and see how they are altered with different interpretations of 'you'.

In successful poems with an unidentified 'you', the connection of the narrator to the person addressed is made obvious by the context. For example, in Margaret Atwood's *You Fit into Me*, the dynamics of the relationship between the narrator, the eyelet, and the 'you,' the fastening hook, are made very clear by the imagery.]

When using 'I' or an unidentified 'you' or any other undefined pronoun in a poem, you need to be absolutely certain that it is the best way of expressing what you want to say.

26

Poetic Philosophy

In the course of our journey to find how to write engaging poetry, we have seen our little example verse:

The wind stirs
bare branches under
a pale morning sky.
Seagulls soar
over the harbour,
wing tips brushing
low cloud.

rewritten over twenty times, each version revised to a different poetic. We have seen everything from the abstract minimal to florid hyperbole – all based on the same verse. The point is that there is no right or wrong way to write poetry. A poem can be written many, many different ways. How do we choose which version to use? We rely on our poetic. A poem is successful in how well it embodies your vision of how language is used to communicate. A poem is the manifestation of a poetic.

As you can see from all these different aspects of the poetic, to be a poet is to be a philosopher – a poetic is a philosophy about language that guides your writing. Our most highly-regarded poets have all been philosophers, not just about language, but in the content of their work as well. They all have something unique to say, a new way of looking at the world and our place in it, and have devised a distinctive language to express their unique view of reality. The content and the form go together.

There are no limits on poetry; there is nothing to say that one way of writing is better than any other. Poetry is not something that can be judged by any objective standard; we can't weigh it, or measure it, or calculate its volume and trajectory – poetry is all made up. The only important standard is your own. But the key to effective writing is the intent: that the way you use the nuts and bolts parts of language – the conjunctions, prepositions, participles, adjectives and adverbs, punctuation marks, similes and metaphors – is intended. There are no accidents in poetry, only intentions. Writing to a poetic will bring integrity and authenticity to your work.

27

The Development of Modern Poetics

After the Norman invasion of England under William the Conqueror in 1066 and the subsequent reigns of the Plantagenet Kings, French culture – and poetry – dominated English culture. The French introduced classical meters and end-rhymes into England. Old English poetry did not use end rhymes, but – since Old English was rich in words beginning with similar sounding syllables – relied on fore-rhymes arranged in alliterative four-beat lines. The adaptation to end-rhyme and meter proved to be very challenging for the English.

The metrical feet of French poetry were designed for long and short syllables of equal stress, a system adapted from classical Greece. In French and other Romance languages, each syllable has the same stress, while in English there are stressed, semi-stressed, and unstressed syllables. The long and short syllables of the metrical feet were replaced by the English stressed and unstressed syllables, but the large vague area of the semi-stressed syllable was left unresolved with the result that most English formal poetry incorporates variant feet.

Also, French depends on word endings for meanings and so abounds with rhyme. Almost any regular verb in French will rhyme with any other regular verb. English, by comparison, is very poor in end-rhyme. The English poets were faced with the task of shoehorning the English language into the French forms – and later into other continental forms, such as the Italian sonnet. Shakespeare was able to modify the Petrarchan sonnet to make it slightly easier to write in English, giving us the Shakespearean sonnet.

The twisting and torturing of English to make it fit the foreign forms sometimes resulted in twisted and tortured meanings. Often, normal syntax had to be inverted in order to end a line on a rhyming word. In *To Rosamond*, Geoffrey Chaucer writes, "

> And like ruby been your cheekes rounde
> Therewith ye been so merye and so jocounde.

The normal syntax is contorted to force 'rounde' to the end of the line to complete the rhyme with the next line. The syntax of poetry became convoluted and complex, often obscuring the meaning of the verse.

One of the standard forms in Old English poetry was the riddle poem. As after-dinner entertainment, the inhabitants of the great hall would recite elaborate riddle poems for the others to solve. The riddles resorted to enigmatic, imagistic and highly metaphorical language, as in this 10th century description of the moon in the sky from the *Exeter Book*,

> By deception it designed
> With pluck and craft, to arc a bower
> High in that airy palace.

In addition, the alliterative form of Old English verse encouraged metaphorical or euphemistic language. For example, if 'the sea' didn't alliterate with the other words in the line, a euphemism would be found, such as 'the whale's road,' a technique called kenning. Similarly, a ship might be referred to as an 'oar steed' or a battle as a 'storm of spears.' While adopting French forms, the English bards retained this colourful and figurative language, as when Shakespeare describes the moon reflected on water in *A Midsummer Night's Dream* as,

...when Phoebe doth behold
Her silver visage in the watery glass..."

English poetry continued to grow in complexity to the point that John Dryden, writing in the late 17th century, complained of the obscurity of John Donne's poetry. John Donne and the Metaphysical Poets, writing around the turn of the 17th century, used complex extended metaphors in ways that almost harken back to the Old English riddle poem.

After that, clarity and consistency of narrative voice began to be stressed in poetry, even though poets continued to jump through hoops to contort the language into metrical rhyming forms. Up until the early 20th century, poetry remained principally narrative and poets, for the most part, made an attempt to write clearly with a consistent voice. The Modernists of the early part of the 20th century largely abandoned narrative and relied on other techniques in the construction of their works, creating a form of indirect associative communication rather than straight-forward story-telling, a form that owes a lot to the dream associations of the earlier French Symbolists and Surrealists.

There was divisive reaction to the perceived obscurity of the Modernist approach and poetry largely returned to the narrative groove. Even later iconoclastic poets such as Allen Ginsberg and Charles Bukowski wrote mainly in a straightforward narrative form. But the lure of non-narrative, associative poetry remained strong and resurfaced in the Post-Modernism of the late 20th century. Again, reactions were extremely divisive leading some poets to retreat into what they considered real poetry, the poetry of rhyme and meter, and establish the New Formalism. The majority of poets went on writing in the established conventional free verse narrative vein while the avant-garde continued to experiment with language, open forms, text and meaning.

One of the criticisms of avant-garde language experiments is the obscurity of the resulting poetry. Obscurity has long been an issue in English poetry. Obscurity in poetry may be unintentional, as when John Milton writes in *On Shakespeare*:

Then thou, our fancy itself bereaving,
Dost make us marble with too much conceiving.

or intentional, as in *r-e-o-p-h-e-s-s-a-g-r* by E.E. Cummings.

Rather than dismissing non-narrative poetry because it is difficult to understand, a productive approach is to try to discern the writer's underlying poetic and ask why a poet would want to write something abstruse in the first place. Language is what we use to communicate, so why would anyone intentionally write something incomprehensible?

The answer has a lot to do with the way language conveys meaning. Language developed as an extension of the associative patterns of our minds. Our minds are constantly attempting to knit the world together and the tool the mind uses to structure reality is association. Our minds are associative engines continually binding our fragmented experiences together into a unified whole. Where there is no association between discrete events, the mind will supply one. Imagine an athlete who wins a competition while wearing a certain shirt. The next competition, engaged while wearing a different shirt, is lost. The athlete then forms an association between winning and the first shirt, the shirt becomes 'lucky' and the athlete won't compete without it.

There is no connection between winning and wearing a certain shirt, but the association is formed by the mind of the competitor. We see this same kind of associative leap in poetry written with disjunctive language – in the absence of the connecting words, the conjunctions, the mind will supply an association between two disparate and unrelated images.

The mind doesn't care if the association is true or not, as long as it makes for a workable framework within which to order experience. Associations which are not supported by physical connections we call belief or faith or superstition or conspiracy theories. Even though they may not be supported by experience or fact, they make the world cohesive and understandable. So powerful is the associative function of our minds that we often find patterns in random elements. It is a recognized psychological phenomenon that, shown a page of dots, a subject will perceive them in coherent groups. The perception of patterns in random stimuli is called apophenia.

Western culture has championed reason as the most important human faculty, but rational linear logic is only one form of association. We also make non-linear connections between objects and events based on emotions, symbolism, apophenia, intuition and imagination. Around the turn of the 20th century, Freud theorized that irrational emotional associations could be created through conditioning. A trauma experienced in childhood could manifest as a neurosis in an adult – the trauma conditioned the emotional response. Ivan Pavlov showed that physical reactions could be conditioned as well when he demonstrated how ringing a dinner bell caused dogs to salivate in anticipation of being fed. There is no physical or logical connection between the bell and the food, but the dogs had been taught to form an association. Most of our thoughts and deeds and attitudes are the result of social and cultural conditioning.

These revelations had profound existential implications: how can we be free if our thoughts, actions and responses are determined by our conditioning? Are we mere automatons forced to perform pre-programmed routines?

One artistic reaction to this psychological trap was Dada which sought to disrupt conditioned responses through the introduction of the random and unexpected.

Surrealism followed soon after with the incorporation of images from the only place where we are free from our conditioning: the natural symbolic language of dreams. If our lives – and even our creativity – are directed by uncontrollable subconscious forces, why not give up the illusion of conscious control entirely and go straight to the source, the subconscious mind? For the Surrealists, psychic events are just as meaningful as physical events and the subconscious is a viable source of both experience and artistic subject matter. Symbolism, as found in dreams, is the natural, innate language of the psyche. That we symbolize before we can talk is evidenced by a child too young to speak who has already formed an attachment to a blanket or stuffed toy – the object is a symbol of security. We have to be taught to speak, but we don't have to be taught how to symbolize.

What is interesting about Surrealist writing is that it is nearly always narrative and syntactical. It uses the conventional meaning structure of language to present startling, and often fun, cascades of images.

As the 20th century progressed, the random elements of Dada and the unconditioned associations of the Surrealists were subjected to various textual and syntactical experiments. Because our minds are so strongly pattern-structured, it is virtually impossible for us to create anything truly random. Everything we imagine has hidden, obscure, conditioned psychic connections.

Besides randomization and dream images, another method of overcoming conditioning and exposing hidden connections is through the disruption of conventional language. The disjunctive language of the Modernists shows how using ordinary words in radical syntax gives us a deeper understanding of the ways in which language conveys meaning. Even though a passage may not make what we would normally call sense, the choice and progression of the words creates an impression or feeling-sense of the meaning. Our shared reality is known only through language – as we cannot read minds, the only way we can know someone else's thoughts, feelings or experiences is if they tell us by communicating through language. By breaking down and regrouping conditioned associations, we can share our experiences in new ways.

Marcel Duchamp dramatically demonstrated this in 1917 when he exhibited a urinal in an art gallery under the title *Fountain*. The lesson is clear: change the context, change the meaning. A urinal in a washroom is a utilitarian object, but in a gallery it is a work of art – the meaning of a thing is defined by its context. This type of shift in meaning-context is something we encounter in our everyday lives: a horseshoe on the hoof of a horse conveys one meaning, while a horseshoe nailed above a doorway will suggest a very different meaning. The object is the same, but its meaning is influenced by the situation in which it is found. Or suppose someone finds out that a trusted friend has been spreading lies; the whole past relationship will be cast in a new light and understood in a new way. Because of the shifts in perception and perspective brought about by that one revelation, the world is irrevocably changed.

These attempts to reframe the elements of our world by putting them into altered contexts and wringing new meaning from the mundane, helping us to experience the world in a new way, provide an approach to modern poetry.

Obscurity is usually associated with our more avant-garde, or experimental, or innovative poets. It is these writers who are forging the way into the future. If writers do incorporate unrestrained abstruseness and nonsense, aimlessly sifting through technical repair manuals to generate poems using six broken wristwatches, the Tibetan Book of the Dead and a 1953 telephone directory from Timbuktu – as some critics have disparagingly claimed avant-garde writers do – who is to say that it is not poetry? Who is to say that a 1953 Timbuktu telephone book is less valid as source of inspiration than any other text or any other experience? The exploration into unusual uses of language is not so confusing when viewed in the context of the history of poetry.

As far back as the 18th century, philosophers such as David Hume and Immanuel Kant were showing us that what we call reality is not entirely discovered through experience, but is largely a construct of the psyche. In addition, the existential philosophers of the early 20th century showed us that there is no meaning, logic or reason outside the human mind – the world is absurd, irrational, chaotic. Things are meaningless apart from the meaning we give them; things are random apart from the order we give them. If poetry is absurd, it is merely a mirror of our reality.

Today's avant-garde, which grew out of this colourful history of philosophy, psychology and artistic expression, continues to experiment with language, form and meaning. Not all the experimental poetry of today will stand the test of time. Much of it will be forgotten. But just because an experiment may not have a lasting effect does not mean that it is not worth pursuing. The truth is that we have no idea what will be considered important in the future. Writing disdained in its day is sometimes revered by later generations: Emily Dickinson is a case in point.

The important thing to remember when approaching avant-garde poetry is that it is intentional: the poets are writing in a non-linear style on purpose. And they are not simply trying to be clever or arty, they are sincerely attempting to push the limits of language. Language is often cut up, twisted and wrung – stretched to the extremes of its frayed edges and beyond to explore how far language can be manipulated and still express something meaningful. Every art-form comes up against the limits of its medium and how artists find ways around those limitations to use the medium for new expression is a defining feature of art.

Avant-garde poetry is an experiment in poetics, an exploration of language. Each poetic is a self-contained schema. A poem created within that structure is meaningful within that frame – and it doesn't have to be meaningful in other frames. The constraints of Romantic poetry don't apply to Beat poetry. This is one of the basic problems with appreciating avant-garde works, that they are often approached with preconceived notions about what a poem should be and about what makes a good poem that are based on older poetics.

There is no one poetic that characterizes all avant-garde poetry. Not all our innovative poets can be said to be attempting to write beyond their conditioning, or exploring the limits of language, or trying to reconstruct language to say things that cannot be said with conventional forms. Some experimental poets stay close to the surrealist tradition and relate bizarre tales in largely narrative, syntactical format. For others, the disruption and disorientation of the language is the message, expressing a sense of alienation by making us feel like strangers in our own culture – a dysfunctional world represented in dysfunctional language. Some intentionally blur the demarcations between the various elements of experience, overlapping inner and outer worlds. Some break their experiences down into basic components and reorder them in new ways. Others use random elements, text symbols rather than words, or invented languages to test the ability of language to convey meaning. Some use surprising juxtapositions of images in an attempt to bypass the critical mind and speak directly to the subconscious. And others provoke alternative perspectives on our shared reality through oblique, lateral, non-linear links rather than direct statement.

With so much variety of personal expression, how do we know when a poem is any good or not? By what standards do we judge it? How do we know we are not being duped into thinking something is great writing when it was really created by chimpanzees clattering away on broken typewriters?

Poetry cannot be judged as 'good' or 'bad' based on its perceived clarity or obscurity. There is no absolute definition by which we can judge poetry as 'good' or 'bad'. Poetry isn't something objective to be found in the world like rocks or trees: poetry is invented by people. The only guide we have for judging poetry is tradition, how others have defined poetry in the past – and it is a changing tradition, constantly in flux. What we consider to be the great poetry of the twentieth century probably wouldn't have been considered poetry at all in the sixteenth century.

Poetry, whether experimental or formal, is either successful or unsuccessful in so far as it expresses the author's poetic, how well it communicates its context, and how insightful, dynamic or unique that context is. Even if random elements are incorporated into a piece, those random elements were consciously added by the writer. The random, the nonsensical, is intended in the work. The random, therefore, becomes purposeful within the context of the artwork; the nonsense becomes meaningful. What is important is not only what the writer presents to us, but the associations between the poetic elements that form in the reader's mind. The reader is invited to create meaningful connections between random shards.

Today's avant-garde writers are building on the basic questions about poetry that other writers have asked in the past: is a poem written without rhyme or meter still a poem? Is it possible to write a poem without conventional punctuation and syntax? Can a poem without a unifying narration or central subject be called a poem? If a poem has no core meaning, is it still a poem? Can a poem be made entirely out of letter forms or glyphs rather than words? Can a poem be taken beyond the limits of the page?

Our experimental poets are not abandoning tradition so much as developing what has gone before. Innovative poets often use the traditional tropes and techniques of simile, metaphor, alliteration, assonance and allusion combined with disjunction, dissociation, radical syntax, idiosyncratic punctuation, abstraction, fragmentation, parataxis, collage and other devices that explore the non-linear processes of the mind, the unconscious processes which provide the emotional, symbolic, apophenial, intuitive and imaginative connections between things.

This is what makes art so exciting and challenging. It is always straining at the limits of what is acceptable, what the materials are capable of expressing, and taking the materials beyond their limitations to present something entirely new and unexpected. Artists are constantly redefining what art is.

The limits of the language keep changing from age to age as our experiences as a society change, and what we have to express about those experiences undergoes change. What was important in one age diminishes while what is important in the next grows and needs to be expressed in new language. Obscurity is redefined in each era; what is judged obscure is a product of the age. John Donne, William Wordsworth, Walt Whitman, T.S. Eliot were radicals in their day, writing about things that had never been written about before and in ways that had not been imagined before – and were all subjected to harsh criticism. But because they are now part of the accepted canon, we forget how innovative they were within the context of their own age.

Poets are continually changing the scope and definition of poetry. Art thrives on change because the world is constantly changing and art must change with it. In order to keep art dynamic and interesting, artists are always pushing the boundaries of their craft; utilizing new materials or old materials in new ways; depicting new subject matter; presenting new ideas, new forms and new means of expression. The obscurity brings increased clarity.

The history of poetry isn't simply a history of great writing; it is a history of poetics, a history of the ideas of what poetry is and the execution of those ideas in verse. It becomes the history of innovation and iconoclasm, a history of the overcoming of the limits of language, a history of expressing the inexpressible – of communicating what the language was not designed to communicate.

Today's poetic experiments are a natural progression from what has gone before. Eventually, some of the techniques developed by today's experimental writers will become more widely used and accepted as legitimate poetic devices. Free verse is an example of this process: fiercely resisted when it was introduced, in time it became the dominant form of the twentieth century. We would not have free verse today if it had not been championed by the avant-garde poets of the past.

Poetry is defined by the people who create it, publish it and read it. Obscurity is in the eye of the beholder. Where the experiments of our age will lead is unknown, but the experimentation is necessary to prepare the way for what is yet to come. It is impossible to lay down rules for where the imagination will go. But we can be sure that poetry will always bring order to the chaos through bringing chaos to the order.

28

Poetic Constructions

Here are some examples of the kinds of poetic constructions often used in free verse poetry today. As you can see, many of them are designed to enlighten through unusual, surprising or unexpected associations. This is by no means an exhaustive list, there are dozens of similar contrivances – you will find that each writer has a set of preferred devices that form the basis of their style. These constructions are not tricks or gimmicks; they are evidence of the writer's poetic in action. Reviewing the techniques used by other writers will help you to be aware of what to look for in your reading and in your own writing:

The small 'I' persona – *example*: 'i am a sailor on an antique sea.'

The reversed adage or common phrase – example: 'afraid of the dark' becomes 'the dark of afraid'; or, 'the wind beneath the door,' becomes 'the door beneath the wind.'

The emotional state couched in technical terms – example: 'The mathematics of sorrow'; or, 'a pneumatic joy'

The negative description – examples. 'her melting was unlike the snow'; or, 'love does not live under stones'

The occasional or accidental or random rhyme in a free verse poem – example: 'they crossed the rocks in stocking feet / while the wind troubled locks of golden hair.'

The use of abstract or indefinite nouns in a concrete or definite sense – example: 'he glued his pride to an infinity.'

The use of casual conversational tics – examples: I guess; I mean; like; and so on; maybe; kind of; etc.

The qualifying of definite or absolute statements – examples: 'I am guilty, maybe.'; or, 'the universe is infinite, sometimes.'

The attribution of unusual qualities – examples: 'the distance of tears'; or, 'the frailty of stars'; or, 'the forgiveness of leaves'; or, 'moments of stone'

The use of nouns as verbs – examples: 'he pewed his fears'; or, 'he taloned her shoulder'; or, 'her memory seizured'

The use of punctuation marks and typographical symbols in place of words – example: [[*]] [#] [!!]

The insertion of foreign, sometimes invented, languages – example: 'he held my hand like a lover./menjadi orang hanya bertahan'

The use of the first line as the title

The reversal or oxymoron – examples: 'a gigantic minimum'; or, 'a tiny sky'; or, 'a sad delight'; or, 'a morose smile'; or, 'a welcome grief'

The unexpected completion – examples: 'a single kiss may result in rooms full of sand'; or, 'the sun veined the pavement, it was a kind of rain'

The building of series of complex words – example: 'a subtle metronomy of ambivalent exigencies questered in antipathies'

The removal of words from a line to change the meaning – example:

I will take you to see my life again
I will take you to see my life
I will take you to see
I will take you
I will take

The invented word – example: 'the crapulescence of futility'

The polysemic usage of words – example: 'she strained the relationship and the tomato soup'

The unusual comparison – examples: 'your words are as beautiful as entropy'; or, 'she is broken like a photograph'; or, 'we fell through our sorrow like light through stained glass'

The unusual modifier – example: 'an invigorate sky'; or 'a supersonic truth'

The strike-out – example: 'the ~~ashes~~ fires are ~~shining~~ deceiving'

The list poem – the items in the list can be related or unrelated

The definite leading to the indefinite – examples: 'We climbed the staircase to an undiscovered future'; or, 'each day becomes a greater fading'

The poem written entirely in lower case, without capital letters

The unpunctuated poem – written without punctuation

The breaking away from the left margin

The rewriting of common phrases – examples: 'up a dry creek without a puddle'; or, 'everything you say will be used in evidence against you'

The unexpected solution – example: 'She wore fishbones over her wounds'

The ascribing of sensuality to emotions – example: 'the spicy smell of sadness'

The negative definition – example: 'A name is no place to hide'; or, 'her softness is not the softness of forgotten moments'

The unusual definition – examples: 'A clock is a candle snuffed'; or, 'the earth is the weight of trouble'

The repeated action – example: 'We dug until our fingers bled / we dug out remorse / we dug up the primal urge / we dug into memory'

The non-sequitur – example: 'there was too much night because all the buttons have been pushed and the scissors are dull.'

The numbered sequence – unrelated stanzas or sections are numbered to give the illusion of a continuous sequence.

29

Literary Terms

Literary terms are humbling because they show us that nearly everything we can think of has been thought of and done before. It may be part of your poetic to use words in unconventional ways and you may think you are doing something unique, until you find out that it has been done so often that there is a term for it: catachresis. The following is only a small selection of literary terms. There are many dictionaries of literary terms available and they make very interesting reading.

Abstraction – the conversion of the physical into the conceptual; to perceive things in terms of sensual elements, such as colour and shape, rather than the physical elements of form and function; to separate or abstract the idea of a thing from its physical form

Alliteration – the repetition of consonant sounds or similar sounding syllables, especially at the beginnings of words

Anaphora – beginning each line or sentence with the same word.

Apophenia – the ability of the mind to perceive patterns, real or imagined, in random stimuli

Association – a subjective connection between things, events, sensations and ideas; associations may be real, supported by fact or experience, or imaginary

Assonance – the repetition of similar vowel sounds

Asyndeton – the omission of any structural words, such as conjunctions, articles and pronouns, that are not essential to the meaning of the piece

Asyntactic – contravening the normal rules of grammar; radical syntax

Atonal – without a unifying overall tone, mood or attitude

Cadence – the natural rhythm of language; the characteristic cadence of a writer is called 'voice'

Caesura – a pause in the middle of a line of poetry

Catachresis – the unusual use of words; to use a word outside its normal or proper sense.

Cliché – a common, usually trite and overused, expression; often used to mean unoriginal, something done many times before

Collage/ménage/bricollage – forms in which various unrelated objects and images are stuck together to create a meaningful whole out of random parts

Conceit – a type of conceptual poetry in which various ideas are linked through a unifying device, such as an extended metaphor

Consonance – using words with the same consonant structure, but different vowels, such as creak and croak; red and rod; blink and blank

Cut-up – a technique in which words or phrases are re-arranged, sometimes randomly, in order to form new and unexpected associations

Didactic – instructive; especially teaching in a moralizing or patronizing way

Disjunctive – language without the conjunctions or connecting words

Dissociation – the breaking of, or denial of, connections between things; the separation of the personality from the world; the inability to emotionally relate to the world

Dissonance – language characterized by the use of discordant sounds

Elision – shortening a word from two syllables to one to make it fit the meter, as in ne'er, o'er

Ellipsis – words missing or left out of the text while retaining the sense, often used to create a fragmented or emotionally halted effect

End-stopped line – a line ending with a full stop

Enjambment – a line which runs on to the next line

Epigraph – a quotation at the beginning of the poem which illuminates the theme or serves as the inspiration

Epiphanic – relating to a great insight, realization or revelation; ecstatically inspired

Euphony – language characterized by pleasant complimentary sounds

Found poem – writing presented as poetry which was not originally intended as poetry; poems have been 'found' in advertising copy, spam emails, textbooks, technical manuals, political speeches and other sources

Fragmentation – to purposely disrupt or deconstruct the normal associations between things; to break events and experiences down into their separate component parts; to see the world in terms of pieces rather than as a whole

Free verse – poetry written without regular meter or rhyme; although free from the conventions of formal poetry, free verse often retains some formal elements, such as metrical elements, regular line length, organization into stanzas, and adherence to the left margin

Glyph – a typographical character; a letter used as a sign or symbol; a letter or character or punctuation mark with a meaning in and of itself rather than as a component part of a written word or syntactical element

Image – an object or word picture used to evoke or represent a thought, feeling or emotion; a sensual representation of an abstract internal state

Inversion – reversal of normal word order, as in "A mouse I thought I saw"

Juxtaposition – putting contrasting or unrelated clauses, images or ideas together

Leitmotif – recurring themes or images which serve to link minor elements of the overall theme together

List poem – also called catalogue verse, in which a number of things, either related or unrelated, are organized into a list, sometimes numbered

Litote – understatement to imply the opposite, as in 'mildly amusing' to describe something very funny, or 'he's so bad' to mean someone is pleasing – also termed meiosis

Metaphor – the description of one thing through the qualities of another, or the identification of two things with shared qualities or properties – metaphors can be simple, as in "He's a pig," or

---

extended, as in equating falling in love to plunging over the edge of a waterfall, cascading through the air and plummeting into the turbulent pool at the bottom

Motif – a recurring theme, image or situation which relates to the overall meaning

Narrative poetry – poetry which tells a story in a straightforward, linear manner

Narrator – the speaker in a piece, not necessarily the author

Neologism – inventing new words

Non-linear – not in an orderly, narrative fashion; breaking the rules and conventions of logic and syntax

Non-sequitur – something that does not logically follow from what has gone before

Objective – concerned with things and events in the world outside the self

Occasional poetry – verse written about or inspired by an event or occasion

Occasional rhyme – also called random rhyme or accidental rhyme – using rhymes that naturally occur in the language wherever they happen to fall rather than as determined by a formal rhyme scheme

Open form – another term for free verse, but often dispensing with all formal confinements, such as regular line length, stanzas and adherence to the left margin; where free verse is free from formal conventions, open forms are open to explore poetic possibilities

Open punctuation – idiosyncratic punctuation; punctuation designed to serve the writer's purpose rather than the rules of grammar

Oxymoron – containing opposite or contradictory qualities; bitter-sweet, an open secret, a cold heat, a glowing darkness, a miserable happiness, a ghastly beauty

Paradox – a contradictory statement which is nonetheless true, such as 'to destroy is to create'

Parataxis – the disjunctive juxtaposition of clauses, often containing disparate images

Pathetic fallacy – the use of natural elements to express human emotions as when a storm rages to show the intensity of someone's anger, or it rains when someone is sad, or the sun shines when someone is happy – 'pathetic' is used in the sense of feeling, as in sympathetic or empathetic, not in the sense of pitiable

Periphrasis – talking around a subject instead of saying what you mean; using unnecessarily convoluted language; using many words to say very little; saying things in a roundabout way; circumlocution

Persona – a fictitious personality adopted by a writer; a persona is sometimes used to view things from a different perspective than the way the writer would usually see them; or to say things that the writer would not normally say; or to express ideas for which the writer does not wish to be held personally accountable

Personification – attributing human qualities or attributes to objects, natural elements, animals, abstract concepts or other entities – also called anthropomorphism

Pleonasm – using unnecessary words, particularly overusing common parts of speech such as than, that, the, etc.

Point of view – the way a situation is seen or described; point of view is usually consistent throughout a work; first person is subjective in which the narrator is 'I'; third person is objective in which the narrator is not involved and relates incidents which happened to others. The narrator may also assume a persona and relate events from the point of view of an invented character. Poetry is subjective when the point of view is personal and objective when the point of view is impersonal, that is, dealing with things in the physical world.

Polysemy – words with multiple meanings; homonyms – often used as puns; the repeated use of the same word with different meanings is called antanaclasis, as in, "He used a hose to hose her hose."

Polysyndeton – the repetition of conjunctions, particularly the overuse of 'and'

Prose poem – poetry arranged in paragraph form rather than lines and stanzas

Simile – a comparison of the qualities or attributes of two things – similes are usually constructed using 'like' or 'as' – deaf as a post, blind as a bat, trembling like a leaf

Sign – an indicator referring to something significant – in some poetics, words are treated as signs rather than units of meaning

Stanza – a group or set of lines within a poem

Subjective – writing concerned with the author's personal, internal feelings and experiences

Symbol – an object, action or image which represents a concept, as when a dove symbolizes peace or giving a flower is a symbolic gesture of love

Synaesthesia –experiencing sense perceptions in terms of another sense, such as perceiving sounds as colours or tastes as music

Syntax – the grammatical structure of language

Theme – the unifying abstract concept or feeling of a work; usually not stated directly, but embodied in the action and images

Tic – a characteristic technique or construction that a writer uses over and over again

Trope – any device in which words are used figuratively rather than literally; simile and metaphor are the most common tropes

Unpunctuated – poetry written without punctuation

Voice – a writer's unique rhythms and usages of language; style

30

Parts of Speech

Poetry is composed of language and to understand language and how it works it is important to know the basic compositional elements: the parts of speech. You don't have to be a grammarian to write poetry, but a general knowledge of the structure of language is helpful.

Words often have many different forms and can be used in different senses. For example, 'sad' can be used as an adjective, 'it was a sad time'; as a comparative adjective, 'it was a sadder, perhaps even the saddest, time for her'; as an adverb, 'she sits sadly by the window'; as a verb, 'she was saddened by her loss'; or as a noun, 'she felt sadness when he left.' These different forms provide us with a great range of expression.

Nouns and verbs

Nouns and verbs form the basic foundation of language. It is possible to communicate, in a limited way, using only nouns and verbs. If nouns and verbs are the basis of language, then it follows that they are the basis of poetry as well.

noun – a noun is a word which represents a thing – and a 'thing' can be physical, conceptual, emotional, sensual, imaginary, ephemeral, spiritual or even non-existent. In language, anything that can be experienced in reality or in the psyche has a corresponding noun. *Book, brick, heat, sky, air, ghost, rabbit, love, fear, state, hero, despair, duty, bravery* are all nouns. It's one of the tricks of language that our feelings and emotions, as well as our ideas, theories and behaviours, are all treated the same as physical objects.

Part of the richness of language is that there are many nouns with similar, but slightly different, meanings and nuances. For example, the noun 'sadness' could be replaced with sorrow, dejection, melancholy, depression, grief, despondency, sorrowfulness, despair, hopelessness, desolation, heartache, misery, unhappiness or the blues. While these words are in some sense synonymous, they all have slightly different connotations representing different degrees or states of sadness. It is important when writing poetry to pay attention to the nouns and not just choose the most convenient or the first one that comes to mind. Study each noun and make sure it is the one you want.

verb – a verb is a word which denotes an action (I do), a state of being (I am), a perception (I feel), a position of ownership (I have), an ability (I can), a possibility (I may), an intention (I will), an imperative (I must), a wish (I would) or an acquiescence (I should). Verbs are the glue that binds the nouns together.

Verbs locate activities in time through the use of different tenses; they embed the time-sense in language. Whenever you use a verb you are establishing an event in time. She sings the song; she sang the song; she will sing the song; she has sung the song; she had sung the song; she will have sung the song; she is singing the song; she was singing the song; she will be singing the song; she has been singing the song; she had been singing the song; she will have been singing the song.

These sentences illustrate the basic verb forms in present, past and future tenses of simple, perfect, progressive, and perfect progressive. There are also conditional, emphatic and auxiliary forms which give us constructions such as: she did sing the song, she may sing the song, she can sing the song, she could sing the song, she must sing the song, she ought to sing the song, she should sing the song, she would sing the song, she used to sing the song, etc. Each tense form describes a slightly different temporal relationship.

While nouns may tell us what things are involved, verbs tell us what is going on with them and when. Verbs also convey intensity and degree of effort. The verb 'walk' has many synonyms which describe different modes: stroll, pace, stride, stomp, hurry, hustle, march, tread, amble, hike, saunter, wander, ramble, trudge, tramp, trek, roam, rove, meander, traipse, shuffle, toddle, etc. Each of these different means of locomotion implies a different emotional state: if someone stomps out of a room they are experiencing very different emotions than someone who wanders out.

The different forms of verbs have different grammatical names. 'To walk' is the infinitive, that is, the root form of the verb from which all other usages are derived; 'walking' is the present participle; 'walked' is the past tense; 'has walked' is the past participle.

Verbs carry a lot of weight. They convey time, physical effort, and emotional intensity. Because verbs communicate so much, when writing it is important to find the verb that best embodies what you want to express. Because our actions and the accompanying emotional states are so varied and complex, verbs tend to be very complex as well with their tenses, participles, auxiliary verbs, active and passive voices, transitive and intransitive forms, and so on. It is this complexity which gives us so much freedom of expression and allows us to utilize the real magic of language.

Descriptors

Descriptors and modifiers help us define our experience. They let us know if an apple is red or green. They inform us if an expression is sullen or cheerful. They can take the commonplace and transform it into something wonderful.

adjective – an adjective is a word that describes or modifies a noun. Adjectives describe physical qualities (red, round), comparative qualities (tall, hot, heavy), perceptual qualities (beautiful, gentle, funny), emotional qualities (angry, sad), quantities (*six* cookies), and type (*car* salesman, *French* bread, *electric* guitar). Adjectives give us a lot of flexibility in the way we describe the world. To say an apple is sweet, delicious, appetizing, nutritious, rotten, bitter, seductive, symbolic, revolting or poisonous provides very different perspectives on a simple piece of fruit.

adverb – an adverb is a word that describes or modifies a verb, an adjective or another adverb. Adverbs are complex words that can tell how, when, where and to what extent. Adverbs allow us to give character to unexciting verbs. To say, "He approached her," doesn't tell the reader much, but we can give a twist to the situation by adding an adverb, as in, "He approached her lovingly, hesitantly, fearfully, cautiously, exuberantly, menacingly, threateningly, confidently." Often the best approach with bland verbs is to find an expressive verb that doesn't need a modifier to get the intent across.

intensifier – an adverb that modifies an adjective or an adverb by indicating extent. These are usually dull words like *very, almost, extremely, quite, rather, somewhat, more, too*. "He approached her too hesitantly, very threateningly, extremely confidently, more menacingly." Intensifiers are best avoided; find intense adjectives and adverbs instead – or better, intense nouns and verbs.

Structural words

The structural parts of speech provide the functional infrastructure of language. If nouns are the buildings of a language city and verbs are the streets, then the structural elements are the water pipes and electrical wires that make the buildings and streets into a liveable environment. And, like the water pipes and electrical wires, we often use them without being aware of them; we take them for granted – it's only when the water or power goes off that we realize how dependent we are on those pipes and wires.

We can imagine someone with a very rudimentary command of English answering the question, "Where are you going?" with a simple verb and noun, "Go store." Someone with a better command of the language might add a pronoun, "*I* go store," then add a preposition, "I go *to* store," then use the present progressive tense with an article, "I am going to *the* store," adding an adjective, "I am going to the *grocery* store," and expanding the sentence with a conjunction, "*and* the hardware store," which finally leads to the composition of complex sentences which communicate so much more than a simple, "Go store": "I'm going to the grocery store, Sweetheart, to pick-up some coffee, which you forgot to buy yesterday when you went shopping, just like you always do, and then I'm off to the hardware store to get a new coffee pot because the old one broke when I threw it against the wall this morning in a fit of anger when I found out there wasn't any coffee."

The problem with structural words is that they are all common, uninteresting, not very pleasant sounding and easily overused. This is the challenge of writers, to use these dull structural words in ways that keep the writing fresh and exciting. Effective use of the structural parts of language is what gives the lilt and music to a writer's voice.

poly-functional words – poly-functional words fill several grammatical uses or lexical categories; for example, *as, this, that, than* can be function variously as adverbs, conjunctions, pronouns, articles or prepositions.

Because of their multiple uses they are often overused and can suck the life right out of a piece of writing. They are best utilized only when absolutely necessary.

article – articles are adjectives that specify particularity: *the, a, an, this, that.* Articles can often be left out without affecting the sense of a sentence. Because nearly all nouns are preceded by an article, they are best omitted whenever possible to avoid overuse.

conjunction – conjunctions are connecting words, they link things together conceptually. Some common conjunctions are *and, but, for, like, or, so, yet.* Conjunctions allow us to compare things, "It's *like* summer today;" compound descriptions, "It's sunny *and* warm;" object, criticize or contradict, "It's sunny, *but* not very warm;" and make many other types of connections. Conjunctions enable us to express the relationships of the different parts of our experiences of the world, both internal and external, to each other. The usage or omission of conjunctions has a profound effect on communication.

preposition – prepositions are relational words. As verbs locate in time, prepositions locate in space. *At, to, from, on, above, in, under, with, near* are just a few of the more common prepositions. Prepositions also define other relationships, such as temporal (*before, after, during, since*) and correlation (*of*). Because they express relationships, and nearly everything we say is related to something else, prepositions are a necessary part of our communication, but they are not very exciting words. It's important to monitor their use closely so that excessive repetition or overuse does not dull-down a piece of writing.

pronoun – pronouns are used in place of nouns. To say, "Bob needed the hammer," is to use the nouns "Bob" and "hammer," but to say, "He needed it," is to use the pronouns "He" for Bob and "it" for the hammer. Pronouns need a context or frame of reference to be meaningful. If a stranger came up to you on the street and said, "He needed it," you wouldn't know what they were talking about. The tendency of pronouns is to make things vague. In common speech we use pronouns loosely and without references because the person we are in conversation with knows what we are talking about, but in writing we are addressing an audience of strangers who may need contextual clues to figure out what is being referred to. If you wrote, "He needed it," you may know that Bob needed the hammer, but unless you tell that in some way to the readers they are going to be left wondering just who needed what?

There are many different types of pronoun: personal (*I, you, he, she, it, we, they, him, her, them, me, us*), possessive (*mine, yours, his, hers, theirs, ours*), interrogative (*who, which, what, whom*), demonstrative (*this, that, these, those*), indefinite (*nothing, everybody, anyone, all, either, many, none*), reflexive (*myself, himself, herself, themselves*), reciprocal (*each other, one another*), and relative (*who, which, that*). They are all vague and should be used with caution – even "I" does not necessarily refer to the speaker, it could be a persona or dramatic character.

Pronouns are prone to overuse. You may have read novels containing a paragraph in which nearly every sentence begins with, "He." "He needs a hammer. He also needs a nail. He is going to hang a picture." There are many ways to get around overuse of pronouns: "Bob needs a hammer and a nail. He is going to hang a picture," or "Bob is going to hang a picture so he needs a hammer and nail," or "He needs a hammer and a nail to hang a picture." As with all parts of speech, be aware of your pronouns and don't let unnecessary particles clutter up your writing.

31

Some Poetics

Here are some of the more important poetic movements that have shaped today's poetry. There are many more groups, factions, sub-groups and splinter-groups than could be listed here, and many influential individual writers who can't be categorized into any particular pigeonhole. All the movements were much more complex and varied than described in these brief, over-simplified blurbs, but the overviews should give some idea of how the ideas of the writers shaped what eventually appeared on the page.

Each poetic expresses a different view of the existential human relationship to the world. Starting with the Elizabethan and Jacobean writers who followed the theory of the ancient Greeks that a person's downfall was the result of character flaws – in other words, we bring all our problems on ourselves – they didn't challenge the society they lived in or question why it was ordered the way it was. Then moving on to the Romantics who saw their lives moulded by grand external forces and rejected social morality for the laws of nature. Then onto the socially and politically conscious writers of the mid-twentieth century who challenged injustice and inequality, using poetry as a vehicle of dissent. And finally to the Post-Modernists who seem resigned to just accept that things are the way they are and no one knows why and that's all there is to it.

In all ages, poetics didn't stand alone, but were part of a cultural milieu, intertwined with other artistic and philosophical movements, sometimes drawing inspiration from developments in painting, music and dance. Twentieth century poetics was influenced by a number of innovative philosophical theories, such as Structuralism, Post-Structuralism, Deconstructivism, and Situationalism. Becoming familiar with these and related philosophies will help in understanding late 20th and early 21st century literature.

Elizabethan/Jacobean Poetry – referring to the late 16th and early 17th centuries during the reigns of Elizabeth I and James I. The writers at this time were not a cohesive group with a shared philosophy, but there are some characteristics of the age that affected later writers. The King James Bible is perhaps the best example of Jacobean writing with its flowing, rhythmical language. The writers of the Elizabethan and Jacobean eras were witty and well-educated, schooled in rhetoric and classical mythology. Writing about religion was forbidden which provided the foundation for a humanist, secular literature, usually involving grand themes and over-riding passions. Some of the major writers of the time were William Shakespeare, Christopher Marlowe, Ben Jonson, John Donne and Edmund Spenser. The language of this age, through the wide distribution of the King James Bible and the works of Shakespeare, has had an effect on all subsequent English literature.

Metaphysical Poetry – John Donne, George Herbert and Andrew Marvell are the best known Metaphysical poets from the early 17th century, during the Jacobean age. Metaphysical poetry is witty and complex, sometimes to the point of inaccessibility. Their main technique is the use of the conceit, a poem based on an extended metaphor to relate some high idea to the mundane world, to relate the part to the whole, to find the eternal in the finite. Donne rarely used nature images or references to classical mythology preferring to focus on human issues like love, sex and death. They wrote in colloquial language and were not overly strict about meter, regarding the form as a vehicle for the content.

Neo-Classicism/The Augustan Poets – poets of the late 17th, early 18th century who emulated classical Roman writers. Their poetry was restrained, conservative, formal, accessible, emotionally detached and written in language almost devoid of metaphor and simile. The proper use of poetry was for satire, philosophical debate, and to mark occasions, not for personal expression. Alexander Pope and John Dryden wrote at this time.

The Lake Poets – often grouped with the Romantics, the Lake Poets, principally William Wordsworth and Samuel Taylor Coleridge, had a distinct voice. With the publication of *Lyrical Ballads* in 1798, Wordsworth and Coleridge introduced a new type of naturalistic, intuitive poetry using common language and portraying ordinary people surrounded by the beauty of nature. Both Wordsworth and Coleridge were concerned with the unseen natural and emotional forces that shape our lives.

Romanticism – the Romantic movement of the early 19th century was a reaction against rationalism and turned to emotion and nature for inspiration. The Romantic world is a mythic place of passion and noble suffering cloaked in heroic beauty. The Romantics didn't deal with social or political issues and completely ignored the seamier sides of life, such as the poverty and degradation of the urban poor. They relied heavily on an idealized understanding ancient Greece as a model for their vision. Their language is ecstatic, grandiose, sometimes over-blown, sometimes exquisitely beautiful. The main Romantic poets are Percy Bysshe Shelley; George Gordon, Lord Byron; and John

Keats. They formed the counterculture of the time with their Bohemian lifestyle, sexual affairs, atheism and drug use.

Walt Whitman – (1819-1892) was never a member of any movement or school of poetry, but he is probably one of the most influential poets in the English language. Whitman was the first to extensively use free verse and wrote in very rhythmical language, reminiscent of the King James Bible. He celebrated the sensual in life, writing exuberantly about himself and showing the heroism of the common man in poetry that is direct, plain-speaking, honest, unsentimental, humanist, egalitarian, socially conscious and sometimes mystical. Whitman single-handedly set poetry on a new path.

Pre-Raphaelites – an artistic movement of the mid to late 19th century, primarily in painting, which sought a return to the simple formality of medieval art before the classical mannerism of the Renaissance. The colours and complexity of nature were coupled with an often morbid sensuality. The main Pre-Raphaelite writers were Algernon Charles Swinburne, Christina Rossetti and William Morris.

Victorian Poetry – with the wane of Romanticism, the poets of the Victorian era in the late 19th century looked to the past to put English poetry back on track. With the heroic ballads of Alfred, Lord Tennyson, Robert Browning's dramatic monologues and the sentimentality of the Pre-Raphaelites, poetry became conventional and unchallenging, serving prudish Victorian sensibilities. Also active at the time were the Aesthetes, who saw art largely as a matter of style and refined taste. They held that the object of art was to present Beauty without any moral or social purpose, although their work often concealed the sensual and decadent sides of life in clever and decorative ways.

The Symbolists – the Symbolist movement originated in France during the latter half of the 19th century, although the Symbolist poets never formed a cohesive group and never referred to themselves Symbolists. Rather than concentrating on the intellectual, classical ideals of the age, such as Truth and Beauty, with the associated sentimentality, the Symbolists focused on the sensual interaction with the world in order to bring emotional depth to human experience by promoting the irrational as opposed to the rational side of our natures in poetry designed to evoke moods rather than depict concrete objects and events. They relied heavily on images and unusual similes or metaphors, sometimes presented in the jumbled way of actual perception, often delving into the darker side of the psyche, which indicated or symbolized the inaccessible and inexpressible inner self. The Symbolists brought the artistic possibilities of free verse forms into prominence. Because of the sensual aspects of their writing they were regarded as decadent and immoral, prone to the perils of the flesh. The main Symbolist poets were Charles Baudelaire, Stéphane Mallarmé, Paul Verlaine and Arthur Rimbaud.

Georgian Poetry – the poets of the early 20th century, around the time of the First World War. They made varied attempts to rescue poetry from the escapism of the Victorian era; some reverted to a sort of sentimental Romanticism, some tried to introduce social realism, most wrote a kind of conventional, formal, popular poetry with strong rhythms expressing middle class values, aspirations and concerns. Significant figures are Rupert Brooke, Walter de la Mare, John Masefield and Robert Graves.

Dada – an anti-art movement that grew out of the insanity of the First World War. The intent was to destroy the bourgeois values and morality that had given rise to the unimaginable horrors of the war. Dada is purposely chaotic, random, nonsensical, offensive and disruptive –

everything that polite society is not. While mainly a visual art movement, its philosophy of intentional destabilization had a profound effect on the development of poetry in the early 20th century. Some Dada artists are Tristan Tzara, Jean Arp and Man Ray.

Surrealism – Surrealism began in Paris in the early 1920s. Assimilating techniques from the Symbolists and Dada, Surrealism confronted the world of the subconscious mind through the use of dream images and free flowing associations. In a search for the truth of existence, the Surrealists ignored common shared reality and concentrated entirely on the workings of the personal inner psyche as the source of all meaning. The movement is best known through the paintings of Salvador Dali, Marcel Duchamp and other Surrealist visual artists. While using vibrant imagery, most Surrealist poetry is narrative free verse that conforms to the rules of grammar and syntax. Some Surrealist writers are Guillaume Apollinaire, André Breton, René Char, Robert Desnos and Paul Éluard.

Imagism – Imagism began in the early 20th century with a group of poets including Ezra Pound and H.D. (Hilda Doolittle). Pound was impressed with oriental poetry and the way the written logograms conveyed the language in discrete units rather than in syntactical strings. H.D. had studied the Greek poet Sappho whose work survives only in scattered fragments. They melded these influences to formulate a poetry which relied heavily on classically-clean imagery expressed in precise language stripped of all unnecessary words. Imagism opened the way for non-narrative verse in English.

Modernism – Modernism is probably the most influential literary movement of the 20th century. It broke with many of the poetic conventions of the time. Modernist poetry is characterized by the use of images, disjunctive language, juxtaposition, parataxis, fragmentation, mythic language, collage, references to classical culture and literature (often in the original language), relentless objcctiviɜm, intcllcctuɑliɜm ɑnd unapologctic obɜcurity. Basically, the language was broken apart and the reader was left to pick up the pieces. Modernism was influenced by the French Symbolist writers, and the Dada and Surrealist artists who followed them, with their reliance on startling, unsettling images. Although the basis of Modernist language was ordinary speech, Modernist poetry often maintained a high, rhythmical, poetic language. The major figures are Ezra Pound and T.S. Eliot. Modernism established non-narrative verse and free verse as viable art forms.

(*Note:* 'Modernism' is a term without a precise definition. It is sometimes used in a broad sense of all 20th century writing before WWII.)

E.E. Cummings – (1894-1962) was not a member of any group, but remains one of the most important writers of the 20th century. He wrote highly individual poetry, initiating many innovations and techniques that would be adopted by later writers. He experimented with idiosyncratic spelling, grammar, syntax, punctuation and typography. Cummings often wrote entirely in lower case, including a lower case 'i', broke lines in the middle of words, mixed up letters, inserted parts of words in the middle of other words, and used spacing and line position in place of punctuation while still maintaining the rhythm of the language. He graphically explored the relationship between language and meaning.

Harlem Renaissance – African-American writers began to assert their voice in Harlem in the 1920s and 30s. They were socially aware and wrote in colloquial, narrative language often incorporating the urgency of jazz rhythms and street jive. The immediacy of the writing and the embodiment of social and political issues in everyday situations, often with underlying anger and frustration, influenced many later writers. The best known of the Harlem poets is Langston Hughes.

The Thirties Poets – sometimes called The Auden Group or The Pylon Poets, although they were never a formal group. The British poets of the 1930s, such as W.H. Auden, Louis MacNeice, Stephen Spender and Cecil Day Lewis, were mostly detached, emotionally remote, formal writers, harkening back to the Georgian poets. Although W.H. Auden was known for the leftist slant of his work, on the whole these writers were narrative, quietist and conservative, writing as if Symbolism, Dada, Surrealism and Modernism had never happened.

The Movement/The Group – some poets in Britain in the mid-20th century who sought a return to rationalism, conservatism and formalism in poetry after the free-form experiments of the Modernists. Prominent names are Philip Larkin, Thom Gunn and Ted Hughes.

Objectivist Poetry – an American outgrowth of British Modernist poetry in the early 1930s – not to be confused with the *Objectivism* based on the philosophy of Ayn Rand. The Objectivists, influenced by Imagism, which was championed in the US by William Carlos Williams, regarded the poem itself as an object, stressing the clarity and sincerity of the poet's vision through the use of simple, everyday language. They rejected the Modernist reliance on classical literature and followed Williams in writing about the world around them, sometimes alternating between the objective and subjective. The main Objectivists poets were Louis Zukofsky and George Oppen.

Black Mountain Poets/Projective Poets – a school of poetry that owes its origins to Black Mountain College in North Carolina, a liberal arts college noted for nurturing innovative writers, visual artists, composers, dancers and designers. The college closed in 1956, but it had a wide literary influence with alumnae writers such as Denise

Levertov turning to political activism while pursuing a distinguished academic career, and Robert Creeley and Robert Duncan becoming involved with the Beats and the San Francisco poets who exemplified the counterculture of the time. Projective Verse, the style for which the Black Mountain Poets are known, was originated by Charles Olson. Olson proposed an open poetry which abandoned the free verse conventions of line and stanza by relying on composition by field in which the layout of the poem on the page was directed by the often fragmented and disjunctive content of one perception leading to another. The basic element of the poem would be the breath unit rather than the line and the rhythm was determined by the poet's ear. Projective verse kept the possibility of non-narrative verse open at a time when most poets were writing in a conventional narrative vein.

Beat Poetry – the Beat Movement began in New York after the Second World War and blossomed in the 1950s with Allen Ginsberg, Jack Kerouac, William S. Burroughs, and Gregory Corso as the main writers. They wrote of the marginalized life outside the American Dream of middle-class suburban living by introducing themes of homosexuality, drug use and mental illness. Their writing was characterized by energetic, spontaneous, loosely structured, ecstatic, consciousness-expanding, unconventional works in everyday urban language that emphasized life in the moment. They were political and social critics who rejected North American morality. Ginsberg and Kerouac turned to Buddhism, a philosophy which influenced their writing. Beat poetry was nearly always narrative free verse.

San Francisco Renaissance – the San Francisco Renaissance poets of the 1950s are often grouped in with the Beat writers and while there was some overlap, the direction of the San Francisco poets was somewhat different. The group melded several influences: Kenneth Rexroth was influenced by William Carlos Williams and oriental poetry; Robert Duncan and Robert Creeley came from Black Mountain College; Lawrence Ferlinghetti came from studying French poetry in Paris, particularly Stéphane Mallarmé. Along with poets like Gary Snyder and Michael McClure, they tended to be more introverted, introspective and nature oriented, writing about themes of personal concern rather than broader social issues. The San Francisco poets celebrated individualism and were varied in their approach to free verse forms. They used colloquial, sometimes hip, language. There was a great variety of style with some writing straight narrative while others wrote non-linear poetry.

New York School – the New York poets were part of a wider avant-garde artistic movement of the 1950s that included Abstract Expressionist painters, jazz musicians and modern dancers. The New York poets were influenced by Surrealism and often presented the ordinary in extraordinary ways. Their work was urban, spontaneous, improvisational, vivid and sometimes abstract, combining narrative and non-narrative aspects. Main figures are John Ashbery and Frank O'Hara.

Confessional Poetry – not a group or movement, but a style of poetry popular through the 1950s and 1960s which centered on the poet's inner turmoil, often concerned with the darker aspects of the personality. This inward-turning poetry was a reaction against the objective stance of the Modernist poets from earlier in the 20th century. While predominantly narrative, the confessional poets applied many Modernist techniques to subjective expression. The best known confessional poets are Sylvia Plath, John Berryman, Theodore Roethke, Robert Lowell and Anne Sexton.

The British Poetry Revival – an attempt, in the 1960s and 70s, to revitalize moribund British Poetry which, by mid-century, had lapsed into an unexciting conservatism. The work of British Revival poets was largely derivative of American movements such as Beat poetry and the New York School.

Post-Modernism – a catch-all phrase for the philosophical, intellectual, social and artistic movements of the late 20th century. Basically it means whatever comes after Modernism. In poetry, influenced by the philosophies of Jacques Derrida, Michel Foucault and others, Post-Modernism is characterized by an abandonment of the need for meaning. Words and phrases are grouped together randomly or to some invented structure of the writer, sometimes giving the illusion of narrative. Alienating, inaccessible, intellectual and objective, Post-Modernism is a kind of surreal Modernism based on the playful interaction of words.

Oulipu – a type of conceptual poetry originating in France in the 1960s, Oulipu is a poetry of constraint. The poet will invent a set of artificial rules, often arbitrary, and then write a poem to those rules. For example, writing without using certain letters, starting every word with the same letter, restricting what vowels may be used, or writing without using the verb 'to be.' An example is Christian Bök's *Eunoia*, which uses only one vowel per chapter.

Deep Image – a reworking of old ideas from Imagism and Surrealism into a new concept in the 1970s. As dream images reveal the true concerns of the psyche, so sensual images reveal the true workings of the world. Deep image poems tend to be lyrical narratives of strung together images, often quite striking. The main writers are Jerome Rothenberg, Robert Bly and James Wright.

Concrete Poetry – a type of writing in which the shape and arrangement of the words and letters conveys the message. There are historical examples of poems with the lines arranged in the shapes of birds or crosses, but Concrete Poetry is usually applied to an abstract style that became popular in the 1960s involving typographical experiments, often using mixed typefaces and letterforms, sometimes using only glyphs or letters instead of complete words to form the poem in order to explore the relationship between written text and meaning. Words and letters are regarded as concrete signs rather than units of meaning. An example of Concrete Poetry is the work of bpNichol.

Visual Poetry/vis-po – a development of Concrete Poetry often combining visual images or picture collages with words, letters and glyphs.

Asemic Writing – text without any semantic content; language abstracted to sometimes illegible forms; letters and words treated as image rather than text.

Mainstream Poetry – sometimes called Centrist Poetry, the style of poetry that predominated the entire 20th century. It is straight narrative poetry usually styled around little stories or vignettes dealing with ordinary people in ordinary situations, often with a moral or life lesson and usually in plain language which, except for being broken into short lines, is indistinguishable from prose. Accessible, conservative, sentimental, it rarely deals with anything too controversial or unsettling. The mainstream writers of the early 20th century tended to be formal, although that gave way to free verse as the century progressed – a conventional free verse that hugged the left margin and was organized into equal-length lines and regular stanzas. Typical mainstream writers are Robert Frost, Elizabeth Bishop, Billy Collins, Ted Kooser and Mary Oliver.

Language Poetry – (sometimes written as L=A=N=G=U=A=G=E poetry after the name of the magazine that promoted it in the early 1970s). Language poets experiment with the forms of language – the significance of a poem is in the language, not in the overall narrative or structure. The concept of the poem and the narrator do not exist, only the line – or sometimes the individual word or letter. A non-linear form, it's rather like combining Projective open forms with Tristan Tzara's or William S. Burrough's cut-up method to force language into unnatural concatenations that the reader may still perceive as meaningful. Major Language poets are Ron Silliman and Bob Perelman.

New Formalism – a movement that rose in the US in the 1980s advocating a return to metrical, rhyming formal verse. New Formal verse is predominantly decorative, concerned with the clever use of language and rarely delving into deep emotion or the existential concerns of life.

Spoken Word Poetry/Slam Poetry/Performance Poetry – came to prominence in the 1980s, Spoken Word poetry is work designed to be recited before an audience rather than read in a book. Usually energetic and rhythmical, it encompasses a great variety of personal styles from rap, hip-hop and dub-inspired pieces to shouted sounds accompanied by expressive gestures. Spoken Word poetry is recited at Poetry Slams, contests in which the poets compete before a panel of judges or for votes from the audience. Performance Poetry is a type of improvisational Spoken Word which is composed on the spot before the audience.

Flarf – a type of absurdist poetry that began around the turn of the 21st century. Flarf is a kind of cut-up/assemblage poetry composed of material gleaned from Internet searches. Some of the assemblages are random, but some are arranged into concocted narratives.

Post-avant – a term without a precise definition – it has been used with many different meanings by many different people. Basically, it is work that comes after Post-Modernism, developing and expanding the experiments of Language poetry in many directions.

Anti-poetry – a term from the mid-20th century with its roots in Dada, 'anti-poetry' has seen a revival by writers who seek to disrupt poetic conventions.

Conceptual Poetry – work in which the idea behind the poem is more important than the actual words, which are often found texts and sometimes nonsense.

Acknowledgements

The example poems quoted in the book, other than those created by the author, are in the public domain. The works suggested for further reading are copyright material. The quotes and further reading suggestions were drawn from the following sources:

The Norton Anthology of Poetry, Third Edition, Alexander W. Allison et al, eds., W.W. Norton & Company, New York, 1983

Poems for the Millennium: The University of California Book of Modern and Postmodern Poetry, Vol. 2: From Postwar to Millennium, Jerome Rothenberg & Pierre Joris, eds., University of California Press, Berkeley, 1998

Howl and Other Poems (City Lights Pocket Poets, No. 4), Allen Ginsberg, City Lights Publishers, Reissue edition, San Francisco, 2001

www.americanpoems.com/

www.poemhunter.com/

www.poetryconnection.net/

www.shakespeare-online.com/

About the Author

John C. Goodman is a Pushcart Prize nominee and the past editor of ditch, (www.ditchpoetry.com), an online magazine of experimental poetry. He has published two collections of poetry, *naked beauty* (Blue & Yellow Dog Press) and *The Shepherd's Elegy* (The Knives, Forks and Spoons Press), as well as a novel, *Talking to Wendigo* (Turnstone Press), which was short-listed for an Arthur Ellis Award. He currently lives in the Gulf Islands, British Columbia, Canada.

This book is also available as an ebook
in Kindle format from Amazon.com